# Leaning Out

The Crikey. Read

# Leaning Out

A fairer future for women at work in Australia

**KRISTINE ZIWICA**

Hardie Grant
BOOKS

Published in 2022 by Hardie Grant Books,
an imprint of Hardie Grant Publishing

Hardie Grant Books (Melbourne)
Wurundjeri Country
Building 1, 658 Church Street
Richmond, Victoria 3121

Hardie Grant Books (London)
5th & 6th Floors
52–54 Southwark Street
London SE1 1UN

hardiegrantbooks.com

A catalogue record for this book is available from the National Library of Australia

Leaning Out
ISBN 978 1 74379 894 2

10 9 8 7 6 5 4 3 2 1

Cover design by Design by Committee
Typeset in Adobe Caslon Pro by Cannon Typesetting

Printed in Australia by Griffin Press, part of Ovato, an Accredited ISO AS/NZS 14001 Environmental Management System printer.

The paper this book is printed on is certified against the Forest Stewardship Council® Standards. Griffin Press holds chain of custody certification SGSHK-COC-005088. FSC® promotes environmentally responsible, socially beneficial and economically viable management of the world's forests.

Hardie Grant acknowledges the Traditional Owners of the country on which we work, the Wurundjeri people of the Kulin nation and the Gadigal people of the Eora nation, and recognises their continuing connection to the land, waters and culture. We pay our respects to their Elders past and present.

# CONTENTS

# AUTHOR'S NOTE

Shortly after the end of the final Melbourne lockdown, in late 2021, Arwen Summers from Hardie Grant sent me a text message. 'I have an idea, do you have time to chat?' At the time I was in Kmart stocking up on essentials for my eldest child who had grown about 6 metres during the lockdown and no longer had a stitch of clothing that didn't make her look like she was about to go digging for clams. 'How about now,' I replied. Within half an hour, Arwen and I were at a cafe across the street mapping out the idea for this book. It was very much a joint endeavour, two women for whom the trauma of working while parenting during some of the world's longest lockdowns was still very real.

We brainstormed with a sense of urgency. There was a story to be told about women and work in Australia, one we believed could have significant implications for the future. Women in alarming numbers were 'leaning out' of paid work, which could have serious implications for their already fragile economic security. And we both understood from our own bitter personal experiences – and those of almost every woman in our sphere and beyond – that women's sanity was equally fragile.

In trying to make sense of what women, both individually and collectively, have been through these past few years, perhaps we could come up with something of value to anyone looking to chart a new course forward for women at work. It would be something that was prepared to tackle the deep structural issues that had long been ignored.

Now, six months later, I have written *Leaning Out*. I wrote it as events were still unfolding, wearing my heart (and my hopes for the future) on my sleeve, and – at times – grappling with the pandemic burnout I describe in this book. I know I can't do justice to the full breadth of women's experiences at work and home, and how the pandemic has exacerbated their distress or inspired them to seek a new way forward. I have tried to produce as accurate a record as possible of what we've just gone through and some of the key insights that experience prompted – in particular, how to remake and renew a feminist discourse in Australia around women and work. But I accept I've by no means covered everything we have learned from this once-in-a-generation event. Where I could, I have looked to history to remind us that many of these fights aren't new, and we stand on the shoulders of giants. And I have focused on the big structural change that languished by the roadside of the high-speed motorway of lean-in feminism that delivered *some* women to their destination, while leaving others behind.

Most importantly, I want us to remember why the rage burned so hot ... and to keep that fire burning.

# INTRODUCTION

Nearly a decade ago, Facebook's chief operating officer, Sheryl Sandberg, published a book, *Lean In: Women, Work, and the Will to Lead*, that became a cultural phenomenon.[1] It had a dazzlingly simple proposition: through sheer will and individual self-empowerment, women could overcome decades of gender inequality in the workplace.

Sandberg's basic premise was that women often hold *themselves* back from reaching leadership positions for a number of reasons, including a lack of self-confidence and concerns about balancing work and family. Her manifesto, part corporate playbook, part bible for her legions of devoted followers, spawned a 'confidence industrial complex' dedicated to teaching women how to 'power pose' their way to the C-suite. It also diverted a generation of women into the fruitless task of forming supportive Lean In Circles, attending workshops to share personal experiences and negotiation tips, and completing post–Lean In Circle meeting homework.

Could there be a more potent symbol for everything that was wrong with lean-in feminism than the idea of women doing the homework necessary to overcome their own oppression?

It was clear from the start who *Lean In* and its particular brand of feminism was for, and who it wasn't. The 'Lean In' woman was typically a high-earning, white corporate woman determined to reach the highest echelons of corporate power.

And it was also clear from the start what kind of advocacy, if any, *Lean In* prescribed: advocacy on one's own behalf. Naked self-interest dressed up as being for the collective good. More than one commentator observed that the solutions *Lean In* offered were highly influenced by the principles of neoliberalism, a form of free market capitalism. *Lean In* ignored the *structural* issues that hold women back and had little to say about how they could be *collectively* tackled.

The publication of *Lean In* came on the heels of the global financial crisis of 2008, which upended global markets and imperilled a generation of men's and women's economic security. It is telling that at a critical juncture in time – a time when a global crisis could have prompted a fundamental reimagining of the systems and structures that shape (and undermine) women's working lives and their financial security – the answer for women came in the form of individual empowerment, and individual empowerment alone.

Now, a decade on, another crisis – the COVID-19 pandemic – has prompted another opportunity for a reimagining. But, too often, women in Australia are still being told to lean in – ironically at precisely a moment, mid-pandemic, when so many are tempted to 'lean out', or have borne the brunt of each wave of COVID that's forced them out of the workplace in far greater numbers than men.

This disconnect between the pandemic-fuelled exodus of women from the workplace, the factors that drove that exodus and the solutions on offer, has been striking. Once again, *Lean In* and the kind of neoliberal, corporate feminism it represented didn't have the answers we so desperately needed.

* * *

As the pandemic has unfolded over the last two-plus painful years, one thing has become clear: data has consistently painted a worrying picture of COVID's disproportionate impact on women, their work, and their ability to earn and save. Women were over-represented in the industries affected by job losses or lost hours,[2] and when schools and childcare shut, women took on a far greater share of the domestic burden of unpaid housework and childcare.[3]

In a study for the *Australian Journal of Labour Economics* economists Leonora Risse and Angela Jackson underscored the extent of that gendered impact.[4] In 2021, women experienced the bulk of the cumulative losses in employment throughout the first twelve months of the pandemic, losing the equivalent of a 55 per cent share of the total months of lost employment despite comprising only 47 per cent of the total employment prior to the pandemic.

As the graph from Risse and Jackson's study shows, the pandemic-fuelled downturn was most definitely shaping up to be a 'she-cession', whereas the global financial crisis was dubbed a 'mancession'. Some even warned that the exodus of women from paid work and the factors driving that exodus could stall, or even reverse, the tenuous gains women had made to bridge the gender gaps in Australian workplaces.

**Figure 1** Change in employment during economic downturns by gender, Australia

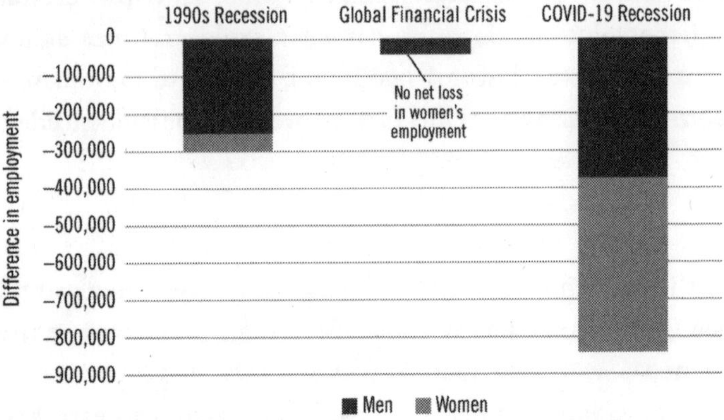

*Source:* Risse and Jackson, 2021. Authors' calculations using ABS Labour Force, Australia. Seasonally-adjusted data series. Net change in national employment measured from the pre-period to the peak of each economic downturn.

Some experts went further, dubbing the economic impacts of the pandemic a 'mum-cession' due to the even more pronounced impact it was having on women with children.

In Australia, the 'motherhood penalty' was already deeply entrenched even before the pandemic. In fact, it was getting worse.[5] This penalty, an umbrella term coined to encapsulate the myriad injustices that contribute to mothers' inequality in the workplace, captures all of the things that have long contributed to a career cliff edge of sorts for too many working mothers, forcing them onto a 'mummy track' of poor pay and poor prospects – if they manage to continue working at all. It includes the 'chores gap': the fact that women shoulder the lion's share of unpaid care and domestic work, the lack of flexible work or equitable parental leave policies for fathers *and* mothers to help level that domestic playing field, the lack of access to affordable childcare, and gender-based discrimination, including pregnancy discrimination.

In September 2021, as the pandemic entered its second year, the unemployment figures again showed that COVID-19 was continuing to have an outsized impact on women's employment. Between May and August, 90,000 women lost their jobs, compared to 25,000 men.[6] In New South Wales alone, nearly two-thirds of all jobs lost since the lockdown in that state began in June were held by women.

What's more, women were more likely to drop out of the labour force altogether – meaning they were no longer counted in employment statistics – with 4.1 per cent of women in New South Wales no longer looking for work compared to 2.8 per cent of men. According to Matt Grudnoff, a senior economist at the Australia Institute, excluding the depths of the pandemic recession in April and May of 2020, the female workforce participation rate had only fallen that sharply once before, way back in July 1988.[7]

And even though women's employment recovered to a large extent after each wave of the pandemic – something the Coalition government was keen to brandish as a victory (job done, nothing to see here, folks) – what might the future hold for women so entirely battered by wave after wave of the pandemic? And what has the pandemic taught us about the fragile foundations of women's working lives? And finally, what have we learned about the fragile state of our care infrastructure, the patchwork of childcare, aged care and disability support services that underpin many women's ability to work? In the absence of these services it usually falls to women to provide that care for free.

'You can dress this up as everything is okay,' Angela Jackson from Equity Economics told me about attempts to paint a rosy sheen on Australia's post-lockdown economic and workplace outlook for women, 'but we know women in Australia are falling behind globally. Rather than focus on the spin, we could act on what the pandemic has taught us about the need for structural reform.'[8]

But would we? Could we?

* * *

Women were 'weary and whiplashed', Associate Professor Elizabeth Hill and Professor Rae Cooper wrote.[9] And they weren't optimistic about the future. According to a Deloitte study published in May 2021,[10] three-quarters of the Australian women surveyed said that their workload had increased since the beginning of the COVID-19 crisis, and close to two-thirds said household commitments had increased too. Job satisfaction had declined from 69 per cent pre-pandemic to 47 per cent. Most worryingly of all, almost one in four women were considering leaving the workforce, with potentially grave consequences for their long-term economic security.

Even before the pandemic, women retired with, on average, half the super of men, and women over the age of fifty-five were the fastest growing portion of the homeless population. Around the world, 'feminised poverty', a term first coined by Professor Diana Pearce, has long been an issue, and Australia is no different. On every measure used to assess wealth and poverty from cradle to grave, women are poorer than men.

As I pondered this bleak outlook for Australian women, I reflected on a January 2020 interview I conducted with Sex Discrimination Commissioner Kate Jenkins about what might lie ahead on the gender equality horizon in the year to come (of course, no one could have seen the pandemic coming).[11] She warned that Australian women were, essentially, in a situation where they would have to fight just to 'hold' the ground they had gained. 'More than in the past, [we] need to keep holding ground as a top priority – we can't take anything for granted.'

By mid-2020, Australian women had decidedly shifted from a situation where they were 'holding ground' to one where they were most certainly losing ground – and fast.

Australia continued its uninterrupted backwards slide in the World Economic Forum's Global Gender Gap[12] rankings, slipping from fifteenth out of 153 countries in 2006 when the ranking was first published, to fiftieth in 2021, a dramatic fall of thirty-five places. But the biggest drop, it's worth noting in the context of the issues I'll canvass in this book, was of fifty-eight places in the women's 'economic participation and opportunity' category – essentially the category that is defined by women's ability to work and earn. Australia dropped from twelfth in 2006 to seventieth in 2021.

And, I couldn't help but notice, there was a troubling correlation between this backwards slide, the emergence of corporate lean-in feminism and the election of a Coalition government at the federal level here in Australia. Almost all of it happened from 2013 onwards.

How did we get here?

A dominant strain of corporate lean-in feminism, unleashed in 2013, coincided with the beginning of nearly a decade of federal Liberal–National leadership. Successive Coalition governments were only too happy to see gender equality exclusively through the narrow lean-in lens of individual women's empowerment while ignoring the broader structural issues. Through this unholy marriage, gender equality, and what might be done to address it, was narrowly defined.

Now, after a decade of thwarted progress, things are changing. Women in Australia are once again embracing a more revolutionary, radical brand of feminism that could – at long last – drive structural change. What has nearly a decade of leaning in and power posing given us? Pilates in a pencil skirt – yes that was a thing! – was of little use during a pandemic when the fragile foundations of women's working lives crumbled and exposed how vulnerable they were.

This was on full display at the Women's Marches in early 2021, when thousands took to the streets in numbers not seen for decades. A generation of younger women – like Grace Tame, Brittany Higgins, Saxon Mullins, Chanel Contos, Nyadol Nyuon, Teela Reid, Moana Hope, Aretha Brown, AJ Clementine (and many others) – were inspiring a more muscular strain of speaking truth to power. And their calls for justice for women soon expanded to include calls for economic justice for women. They took on issues for women at work that had, in the past, fallen outside the focus of corporate feminists.

And yes, women were angry, and rightly so. And maybe that anger makes some a bit uncomfortable after a decade of more palatable, pink-washed, corporate feminism.

But here's the thing about the 'angry feminist' trope. It's actually quite useful to be angry, despite what some feminists would have us believe, the kind who spend their lives suppressing overt expressions of their rage, lest they be tarred with the 'angry feminist' brush.

A 2014 article in *Psychology Today*, 'Go Forth in Anger', highlighted a growing body of research from social and evolutionary biologists, psychologists and brain scientists that dented the long-held view that anger is a negative or destructive emotion.[13] Anger can be a force for good, the research showed, decreasing levels of the stress hormone cortisol, thereby helping people calm down and get ready to address a problem. According to researchers, anger is an 'approach emotion' that fuels optimism, creative brainstorming and problem solving by focusing the mind and mood in highly refined ways. It's the opposite of fear, sadness, disgust and anxiety, all feelings that prompt avoidance.

But anger and its associated benefits have been – until recently – denied women, in particular Black women and women of colour. Just a year later, *Psychology Today* published another article, 'Why Don't We Trust Angry Women?', which highlighted new research that found women who expressed their anger in impassioned speeches intended to persuade others were less likely to get results compared to men.[14]

As someone who has spent nearly two decades campaigning for change armed with data and a hefty side order of calm, I've been feeling the benefits of a fuel injection of anger.

We've made 'the case for change'. Now it's time to demand it.

And that anger has also stirred another powerful emotion, hope. But not hope in the passive sense, hope in the active sense. As Rebecca Solnit wrote, 'Hope is not a lottery ticket you can sit on the sofa and clutch, feeling lucky. It is an axe you break down doors with in an emergency.'[15]

To my mind, the millions of angry women now speaking out have wagered on the power of their experiences, the power of their voices to serve as the axe that breaks down doors.

Australians and Australian women have lived through an incredible two and a half years of disruption – and change. The lessons we learn from this pandemic era and how we apply them to the ongoing project of gender equality and women's economic security could have profound implications for the future.

From my own misadventures in power posing, to the death of the #GirlBoss, from the home front to the work front (including daily skirmishes with persistent discrimination and a lack of workplace safety), we'll tackle it all in this small but mighty book, landing on what I hope will be a new deal for women at work in Australia. If we don't ask the big questions now, explore how we got here, and map out an alternative way forward, we risk repeating the mistakes of the past and, in the words attributed to Winston Churchill, 'wasting a crisis'.

We are at a crossroads. What can the world of work look like? Who can participate and on what terms? The pandemic has dramatically changed our ideas about what's possible, upending almost a decade of stasis when we looked at these issues through a narrow lens. From crisis comes change.

# 1.

# WHEN GIRL POWER GROWS UP

Nearly a decade ago, I arrived in Australia after stints working on the issues of gender equality and violence against women as both a journalist and an advocate in the United States, Germany and the United Kingdom.

These countries clearly have their own chequered histories with gender inequality, and provide examples of both high and low moments in feminist activism. But when I arrived on Australian shores I was genuinely puzzled by much of what passed for mainstream feminist discourse and activism here. Australian feminism was dominated by a strain of white, neoliberal 'female empowerment' that had gone out of style elsewhere, or, at the very least, wasn't permitted to take up so much prime real estate within 'the movement' without significant challenge. Meanwhile, I observed that Australian feminist institutions that could have taken up a more robust fight had been actively undermined.

A few of what I'll call my 'misadventures in power posing' illustrate the point, as the constraints of this new reality slowly sank in.

There was the time, years ago, when I first met with advisors to Sex Discrimination Commissioner Kate Jenkins at the Australian Human Rights Commission. I described to them my work at the UK's comparable body, the Equality and Human Rights Commission, which included advocacy campaigns and robust enforcement actions. One advisor leaned over to the other and whispered, 'Real teeth' – something, I would soon realise, that the Australian body found difficult to exercise without fear of repercussions. Advocacy in particular, I would come to learn, is a big no-no in much of the government-funded Australian women's sector.

I was not surprised when a few years later, in March 2020, the Australian Human Rights Commission had to cut one in three jobs due to inadequate funding by Coalition governments. According to the Commission, the current funding did not 'provide us with resources to perform our statutory functions'.[16]

Nor was I surprised when – a month later – it emerged that the Commission was at risk of losing its 'A-status' from the Global Alliance of National Human Rights Institutions because of the way successive Coalition governments had appointed commissioners. Instead of an open, merit-based selection process, governments had used 'captain's picks', which could, arguably, undermine the integrity of the Commission from the inside.[17]

And, as I said, 'advocacy' is a giant no-no for much of the women's sector, which relies on government funding; if you speak out, you risk losing funding. An example: in July 2021, the Morrison government defunded the Security4Women Alliance, one of the six national alliances funded by government that had been raising the issue of women's economic security for more than two decades. Had the Alliance got a bit too big for its britches by saying too many inconvenient things about women's economic security? 'It's just grubby,' Judith van Unen, the co-founder of the Alliance, told me. 'There's a silencing by stealth, not inviting you to a critical meeting or not renewing your funding.'[18]

Mainstream feminism had taken on a corporate vibe – like the time I went to an event run by a high-profile women's networking company. After sitting through an 'inspiring' speech delivered by a white woman who had reached the apex of her career and assured the rest of us that we, too, could follow in her footsteps, I left with a pink goodie bag adorned with the slogan 'My super-power is being a woman'. Inside the bag was an advert for the new Corporate Barbie. I dumped it in the trash as soon as I left. (I kept the posh herbal tea. What? I'm only human.) This particular, highly lucrative speaking circuit had seemingly become a way for some high-profile women to manifest their feminist credentials while also profiting from them.

And then there were the successive International Women's Day celebrations, usually an obscenely early breakfast. At dawn, we do feminism! I wondered where the radical spirit was among the sea of pink-washed breakfasts served up alongside pink cupcakes and more 'inspiring' you-can-do-it, rah-rah lean-in mantras. My heart sank each year at the sight of countless women donning their 'The Future is Female' T-shirts, accepting the paltry crumbs from the table that a single day to discuss their issues offered … and then only through the narrow prism of what women *themselves* could do to fix it.

Did anyone at any of these events ever remark on the fact that the Australian Human Rights Commission published a report in 2014 that found one in two mothers experienced pregnancy-related discrimination? And that the report's four key recommendations were ignored by successive Coalition governments?[19] It was at one of these breakfasts that the then prime minister, Scott Morrison, infamously said that the Liberal Party wanted to see women rise – but not at the expense of men.

And finally, there were the countless organisations set up specifically to advance gender equality almost exclusively through the narrow lens of the 'business case' (do it because it's good for business, not because it's the right thing to do). And what, predictably, flowed from the singular pursuit of change on those terms alone. I confess that I myself had played the 'business case' game in seeking to persuade, but I was increasingly disillusioned.

For example, in 2017 the Male Champions of Change (they have since rebranded as simply Champions of Change, perhaps in recognition of the fact that giving men top billing for doing the bare minimum has reached its use-by date) issued a press release proudly proclaiming that their members had 'pledged' to eliminate 'like for like' gender pay gaps at their organisations. 'Like for like' – in plain English – means paying Bob and Sally differently for doing *the exact same job*. Dear Reader: this has been illegal for fifty years.

While the 'pledge' received glowing media coverage in the majority of the Australian press, I put my hand up to cry foul. In my regular column for *Women's Agenda* I voiced my disbelief at the situation: are you kidding me? The male CEOs of some of Australia's biggest organisations just 'pledged' not to break the equal pay law that has been the law of the land for nearly 50 years and we're congratulating them?[20]

I later received a report from Future Super that asked ASX 100 companies whether they would *voluntarily* increase transparency and publicly report the size of their gender pay gap, as was already the law in the UK.[21] And when I cross-referenced those who said 'no' with ASX 100 companies whose CEOs were Male Champions of Change, I was not impressed: roughly half said 'no'.

These are but a few examples. I could go on, I assure you. And I know, I'm a bit of an Eeyore. (I will brighten up eventually, I promise!) But I've taken you on this trip down memory lane to highlight how farcical – and downright hollow – much of the mainstream gender equality 'advocacy' had become in Australia.

To really understand how we got here, we have to go back a bit further in our feminist time machine to the mid-1990s. The era that saw the birth of Girl Power. Sometimes things are a bit clearer through the rear-view mirror.

* * *

The history of feminism is often talked about in terms of distinct 'waves'. While this is, admittedly, a bit reductive, and each wave of feminism was not a monolithic movement, it's still a useful tool to understand the movement's history, where it came from, and how it developed.

The first wave took place in the late nineteenth and early twentieth centuries, emerging out of the push for female suffrage, the West's first sustained movement dedicated to achieving political equality for women. This wave formally began at the Seneca Falls Convention in the United States in 1848 when 300 men and women rallied to the cause. And for seventy years, the so-called 'first-wavers' marched, lectured, protested and hunger-striked their way to the vote. They also pursued equal opportunities in education and employment and the right to own property. On 18 December 1894, the South Australian Parliament passed the *Constitutional Amendment (Adult Suffrage) Act*. It not only granted women in the colony the right to vote but also allowed them to stand for parliament. Later, the *Commonwealth Franchise Act 1902* allowed non-Indigenous women in all states to vote and stand as candidates in federal elections. Yes, progress, but indicative of the racism and willingness to prioritise some women's progress at the expense of others that characterised the first wave.

The second wave began in the 1960s with the publication of Betty Friedan's now iconic *The Feminine Mystique*, which came out in 1963 in the United States and sparked a cultural phenomenon by famously describing 'the problem that has no name', the unhappiness of a generation of housewives who had been encouraged to return to hearth and home after the Second World War. As Constance Grady wrote in *Vox*, Friedan's book gave women 'permission to be angry' and rallied them, once again, around a unifying feminist goal, this time to fight for not just political equality but social equality.[22] Second-wave feminism brought legislative change in Australia, including the criminalisation of rape in marriage and the decriminalisation of abortion, and it became illegal to pay a woman less for doing the same job as a man.

Women also gained access to paid maternity leave, childcare and domestic violence refuges.

The third wave began in the mid-1990s and was influenced by two things: the Anita Hill case in the United States in 1991 – in which Hill accused Supreme Court nominee Clarence Thomas, who had been her boss in two government jobs, of sexual harassment at work; and the riot grrrl groups, and the music and 'zines' (homemade magazines) that grew up around that movement. Young women watching Anita Hill's case were galvanised to tackle some of the unfinished business of the second wave with renewed vigour, while also reshaping feminism for a modern time, including seeking to make it more inclusive and, the buzzword then and now, 'intersectional'.

'I am not a postfeminism feminist,' declared Rebecca Walker (writer Alice Walker's daughter) in a 1992 article for *Ms.* magazine, in which she gave the budding movement a name: 'I am the Third Wave.'[23]

It was this moment in time, the dawn of the third wave, that was foundational to my feminist awakening, and what led me, four years later as an undergraduate at New York University's journalism school, to seek an internship at *Ms.* magazine, an experience that gave me a firm foundation (and lifelong friendships) for my career and advocacy that was to follow.

But then things started to get a bit complicated with the arrival of Girl Power.

The term Girl Power was first credited to the US punk riot grrrl band Bikini Kill in 1991 and grew up out of the third wave, but it was later popularised by the British girl group the Spice Girls in the mid-1990s.

Bikini Kill's frontwoman, Kathleen Hanna, was famous for calling out 'girls to the front' at gigs, a symbolic gesture that offered women at their concerts both a platform and safety. The 1980s had been a bruising decade for feminism, well documented in Susan Faludi's *Backlash,* which gave the phenomenon a name. All the ills that befell women and society were blamed on 'angry', 'hairy-armpit' feminists: childless, it's because you left it too late to pursue a career; stressed and unhappy, it's because you're trying to 'have it all'; left your kids at childcare, did you know they're staffed by paedophiles? The 'spicified' version of Girl Power offered a way forward, an opportunity to rebrand feminism and entice the next generation, in theory at least, back to the barricades.

'It's like feminism, but you don't have to burn your bra,' Geri Halliwell, aka Ginger Spice, boldly proclaimed. 'We're freshening up feminism for the 90s.' There were five Spice Girls, each with her own niche brand: Halliwell, plus Melanie Brown (Scary Spice), Victoria Beckham (Posh Spice), Emma Bunton (Baby Spice) and Melanie Chisholm (Sporty Spice). They portrayed themselves in public and in film clips as devoted to each other, a girl gang that was cheeky and playful, and didn't take male power too seriously, as when Scary Spice planted a big kiss on Prince Charles. 'You've got lipstick on you now,' she said. That proved a prescient comment. We all had lipstick on us now, as this new brand of feminism was very encouraging of more traditional expressions of femininity that the second wave had, stereotypically, jettisoned.

In the Spice Girls movie, *Spice World*, Scary Spice scares a potential lover by saying the word feminism … wait for it … out loud. As he runs away, she joins the other Spice Girls in raucous laughter. I suppose this cinematic interlude says a lot about the perceived 'brand value' of feminism post-1980s and the widespread belief that it badly needed a refresh.

'No way we're gonna stay at home and do washing up for some man ... he can take me out for dinner,' proclaimed Brown. What a simple solution to the unequal division of domestic labour between women and men. We can all go out to dinner! Except many of us don't have the privilege of dining out regularly as a solution to our domestic woes, and what about the wages and conditions of those who dish up that dinner? Or clean our houses for us? Or mind our children? (We'll return to this in Chapter 2 and 5.)

Feminist academic Katharine Coman has described Girl Power as a 'jumble of feminist insights and hopes'. But at its most simple, the issue was that Girl Power and feminism defined the problem and the solutions very differently.[24]

'Girl Power' refers to an attitude that women and girls should be confident, make choices and achieve things independently of men. 'Feminism', on the other hand, is the belief that women should be treated the same and permitted the same rights and opportunities as men. Notably, feminism also involves taking action to achieve this state.

There are a few subtle but important differences between these two definitions. One is that Girl Power was never particularly focused on *how* women might achieve things independently of men, the vitally important 'action taken to achieve this state'. It was just about showing up with your T-shirt and swagger. Girl Power was focused on the individual quality of 'confidence'. From Girl Power, *Lean In* would be born.

Girl Power was 'like' feminism, but it wasn't really feminism at all. It didn't interrogate the power dynamics between the sexes. It didn't examine the structures in which those dynamics operate. It didn't ask hard questions about privilege, class and race, and who gets to benefit from the 'power' part of Girl Power in a deeply classist and racist society – and who doesn't.

Those of us who came of age in the 90s (present company included) were sold a pup. And I can't emphasise the word 'sold' enough: Girl Power was a product that was sold to young women in the form of merchandise, alongside the promise that the hard and necessary work of confronting structural inequalities and power imbalances needn't happen. You could be a feminist, but a 'friendlier', less scary version who didn't hate men, wore make-up and got everything you wanted in life.

Women of this generation were lulled into a sense of complacency that Girl Power did nothing to disrupt. The Girl Power generation could take the previous generations' feminist achievements for granted. Was there a great feminist fight for us to embark on collectively? Or were we now, as *individual* girls, the great feminist project? Yes, indeedy, we were.

'The problem is – the problem has always been – that feminism is not fun. It's not supposed to be fun. It's complex and hard and it pisses people off,' wrote Bitch Media co-founder and author Andi Zeisler. 'The root issues that feminism confronts – wage inequality, gendered divisions of labour, institutional racism and sexism, structural violence and, of course, bodily autonomy – are deeply unsexy.'[25]

But what happens when Girl Power – and the girl power generation – grows up?

* * *

In October 2003, a decade after Girl Power came to prominence, *The New York Times* published a cover story that provided a tidy explanation of why many of the ambitions of the Girl Power generation hadn't translated into career success. By this point, those of us who had been sold the lie that we could do or have whatever we wanted had some questions.

In her article, 'The Opt-Out Revolution', Lisa Belkin asked: why don't more women get to the top? The answer: they choose not to.

Emphasis on 'choose'. Women were simply 'choosing' hearth and home over their careers, and thus so-called 'choice' feminism was born.[26]

Other similar news stories followed, including a *Time* magazine cover story on 'The Case for Staying Home' and a US *60 Minutes* segment devoted to a group of former mega-achievers who were, as the anchor Lesley Stahl put it, 'giving up money, success and big futures' to be home with their children.

This moment in time was captured in the television series *Sex and the City*, when Miranda, one of the main characters, questions her friend Charlotte's 'choice' to give up her much-loved job at an art gallery following her marriage, to concentrate on her new role as a wife and, one day, a mother. Charlotte is offended and demands Miranda's support. The women's movement is all about women having 'choices', she lectures Miranda, before shouting repeatedly, 'I choose my choice.'

The exchange came to represent everything that was wrong with 'choice' feminism, the latest iteration of feminism offered up to explain a lack of progress and make everyone feel better. There was little questioning of who has 'choices', and whether women who operate in an environment of constrained choices (say, due to unaffordable childcare, a lack of flexible work, an unreconstructed partner who doesn't do their fair share at home) really have a choice at all.

But more importantly, the movement perpetuated this idea that anything, absolutely anything, a woman *chooses* to do is feminist just because she, a woman, chooses to do it. This would later give way to the idea that as long as an individual woman is 'empowered', that's feminism … it doesn't matter how she wields that power. Nor does it matter if her individual success masks a lack of change for the majority.

Ten years later, in 2013, *The New York Times* ran another story, 'The Opt-Out Generation Wants Back In'.[27] Faced with divorce, financial hardship, lack of fulfilment or all of the above, the women of the Opt-Out Generation were anxious to get their careers back on track – and, not surprisingly, many were finding it very difficult.

Linda R. Hirshman, retired Allen/Berenson Distinguished Visiting Professor of Philosophy and Women's Studies at Brandeis University, foresaw this outcome. In her book, *Get to Work*, published in 2006, she mercilessly took this generation of over-educated and, in her view, underperforming women to task, assailing the 'useless choice feminism' of an 'I gotta be me' generation.[28]

But I wonder if Hirshman's ire would have been better focused on the systems and structures that constrained women's choices – and the dominant media and cultural narrative that sought to persuade women that they were actually, to paraphrase the immortal words of Charlotte, choosing their choices.

Joan C. Williams, an academic at the University of California's Hastings College of Law Center for WorkLife Law, published a study that same year entitled '"Opt Out" or Pushed Out? How the Press Covers Work/Family Conflict'.[29] The study, co-written by Jessica Manvell and Stephanie Bornstein, unpacked some of these questions, exploring why the story kept coming back time and time again, with selective statistics and misleading anecdotes exclusively drawn from white women in the upper echelons of society. The answer: because these women parroted conventional, comforting, traditional ideas about gender roles. 'And here's why that matters,' wrote Williams and her co-authors. 'If journalists repeatedly frame the wrong problem, then the folks who make public policy may very well deliver the wrong solutions.'

Yes, they will.

2013 also saw the publication of Sheryl Sandberg's *Lean In*, the multi-million-copy-selling bible of corporate feminism that encouraged women to 'choose' to lean in – precisely the wrong solution Williams and her colleagues warned of.

And hot on its heels, the #GirlBoss was born. American Sophia Amoruso, then in her early twenties, had turned her eBay account into a fashion empire called Nasty Gal, and her pop feminist memoir, also titled #Girlboss and published the year after *Lean In,* sold more than half a million copies. By 2017 she had founded Girlboss Media, devoted to helping millennial women 'progress as people in their personal and professional lives'. The movement was well underway.

The proposition was simple. Young women would not ask for but would take their seat at the top table. They would lay claim to the power, and as the evangelists of the #GirlBoss way believed, a high tide would lift all boats.

To #GirlBoss became a verb.

There were just two problems. Firstly, the belief that a high tide (of some women) would lift all boats just wasn't true. Women, collectively, needed to tackle the broad abuses of power and structural issues that failed the many, not seek escape hatches, or exceptions, for the few. And we should never assume that women are by their very nature better than men and immune to the malignant influence of power and the pursuit of profit above all else. In the last few years, a number of media reports have documented the concerning labour practices and hypocrisy of a number of #GirlBoss icons, including Amoruso herself.

In Australia, the Coalition toppled Kevin Rudd's Labor government in 2013, the same year *Lean In* was published. The new government embraced the neoliberal principles of individual merit and empowerment that lay behind lean-in feminism and the #GirlBoss. Inertia on gender equality was the result. Every major government policy document on gender equality over the next ten years, including the 2022 Women's Budget Statement, reinforced the status quo.

As became my habit, I checked the Statement to see the number of times the word 'choice' appeared versus the word 'discrimination', my litmus test for the extent to which the Coalition government understood the drivers of gender inequality and the necessary solutions. The results were, as they always were, dispiriting. The word 'choice' appeared fourteen times, while 'discrimination' featured just seven times, and four of those were repeated references to the sex discrimination commissioner's job title. Clearly, this was a government that was sending a powerful message that gender inequality was down to women's 'choices' and it could be tackled by lean-in solutions aimed at 'supporting' women to 'train', 'boost' and 'revive' (actual words from the statement) their own way out of it.

This was the context in which we found ourselves in the summer of 2020 when the pandemic arrived on Australian shores. Little did we know what lay ahead. That the pandemic would upend this. That the emergence of two extraordinary young women, Grace Tame and Brittany Higgins, onto the national scene would upend all 'the rules' about 'how we get things done' in relation to violence against women and gender equality in Australia.

The need for 'quiet' conversations 'behind closed doors'. The demand to be 'civil' and 'constructive' at all times – to never rock the boat. And to never, never partake in full-throated advocacy lest we upset our political paymasters. These expectations were being overturned thanks to figures like Tame and Higgins.

The more recent times we've lived through have exposed Girl Power, choice feminism, *Lean In* and the #GirlBoss for the false dawns they were. In 2022, are we ready to shed these veneers of faux feminism? I think we are.

# 2.

# WHO CARES? FROM CAREER FEMINISM TO CARE FEMINISM

On 11 November 2021, Sam Mostyn, an independent company director, long-time women's advocate and current president of Chief Executive Women, arrived at the National Press Club to deliver what would subsequently be hailed as a landmark address.

Mostyn promised to deliver insights from 'a relentless two years during which women had been trying to deal with the upheaval to their world caused by COVID'. And she promised to extrapolate from those insights some key lessons regarding 'what Australia could – and should – look like as we emerged from one of the most disruptive and challenging periods in our history'.

Given the disproportionate impact the pandemic had had on women, and given Australia's relatively recent feminist reawakening that culminated in the March4Justice rallies across the country, it came as no surprise that Mostyn was offered such a prominent platform at the National Press Club to canvass these issues and chart a course forward.

Many listeners – if not most – were probably expecting a speech that focused on the more traditional Chief Executive Women territory of women in leadership and women on boards, the kinds of issues that have topped the corporate feminist agenda for more than a decade. But Mostyn had a radical surprise in store: she would have a laser-like focus on care, the so-called 'care economy' and 'care infrastructure', in particular the low pay and poor conditions that are hallmarks of the care industries dominated by women, including aged care, early years education and care and disability support services.

Mostyn framed her remarks in terms of Australia's iconic characterisation as a Lucky Country. 'In Australia, we like to tell ourselves that we are the Lucky Country … and yet among our vast natural resources, possibly the most underrated, undervalued has been the unpaid (and low paid) work of women,' she said. 'We are "lucky" to have benefited from that for so long.'

'We virtually never hear how care and economic performance and success go hand in hand,' Mostyn added. 'They are inextricably linked, and they are the foundation of our future prosperity.'

The gauntlet was thrown down. The whole purpose of Mostyn's speech, she said, was 'to put care at the centre of the economy'. Watching at home, I was blown away.

To my mind, Mostyn's speech represented a turning point for Australian feminism, a transition from the lean-in, 'career feminism' that had dominated mainstream Australian feminist discourse for nearly a decade to a 'care feminism' that grappled with the critical role that care, and care infrastructure, plays in our economy – it is the work that makes it possible for other women to work. It is also, according to the Grattan Institute, a larger and larger portion of the economy with each passing year, with most jobs growth over the next five years expected in services industries, where 90 per cent of women already work (most of these jobs are in healthcare services).[30] What's more, there's expected to be far fewer jobs in the more traditional male-dominated industries of agriculture, manufacturing, construction and mining. The economy has been changing before our very eyes, though it seems some people haven't noticed.

Mostyn's point was that this is the future of the economy, and there is a lot to be gained – from both a social and economic perspective – by facilitating a long-overdue shift in how we think about care. Comparing a $1 million public investment in education, health and construction, the progressive think tank the Australia Institute has estimated that the employment boost from that stimulus in male-dominated construction is minimal (only 1.2 jobs) compared to the female-dominated health sector (10.2).[31] That's a ratio of ten jobs in education and care to one in more traditional 'infrastructure' for the same amount of stimulus investment. Yet the Coalition government – at the height of the pandemic – continued to direct all the cash stimulus towards traditional 'hard-hat'/'hi-vis' industries, with women missing out. It would seem the Coalition government had no shortage of hard heads donning hard hats.

Mostyn was also keen to explore the appalling way we as a society don't value the critical caring work women do simply because women do it. We are missing out in terms of reaping the social dividend of increased community wellbeing, and the human capital formation and productivity dividend, boosting long-term productivity by freeing up more people, usually women, with caring responsibilities to work.

Mostyn clearly understood that the women who do the unpaid and low-paid caring work might have zero interest in 'leaning in' to the corporate leadership roles typical of members of her organisation. And thank bloody Christ they didn't subscribe to that singular definition of workplace 'success' for women. Because without our care workers, we would live in a society that doesn't provide even the minimum standards of care to our disabled and ageing loved ones or the best start in life for our children.

It was high time women in executive roles showed they had the backs of the largely female care workforce. A bit of good-old fashioned feminist solidarity – to my mind – was long overdue.

In a 2021 essay for *The New York Times*, Anne-Marie Slaughter, chief executive of the New America think tank, made a similar, scathing observation about the care economy and care infrastructure, in particular the extent to which they had *not* been on the agenda of women in executive roles. Entitled 'Rosie Could Be a Riveter Because of a Care Economy', Slaughter's *NYT* piece scolded the more recent generation of corporate feminists for not paying enough attention to care.

'The value and visibility of care goes far beyond the definition of infrastructure. It is the central question of 21st-century feminism, and one far too long ignored or downplayed not only by men but also by many prominent women, particularly wealthy white women who have been able to leverage the privilege of race and class,' wrote Slaughter. 'Care feminism has long taken a back seat to career feminism. Advocating for child or elder care may be less glamorous and newsworthy than breaking glass ceilings to become the first woman in a role traditionally reserved for a man, but both are necessary if we are ever to achieve true gender equality.'[32]

Mostyn's speech represented the brave new vanguard of care feminism in Australia, and a very welcome break from the dominant career feminism. And this new era of care feminism was, by its very nature, intersectional. Migrants make up a significant and growing proportion of the aged care workforce (35 per cent) in Australia, for example, and research has found that migrant home care workers from non-English speaking backgrounds are more likely to be employed on a casual basis and report hours related underemployment.[33] By taking up the cause of care, care feminists were also taking up the cause of the many women from culturally diverse backgrounds who work in this undervalued profession.

The vital issues of the value of care *and* the value of women's paid and unpaid care work were, at last, moving from the fringes of the debate to the centre. And the fact that this unequivocal message was coming from the president of Chief Executive Women, an organisation traditionally associated with career feminism, was symbolic of how mainstream care feminism was fast becoming – and the impact it could have.

But there were, as there always are, trailblazers who laid the groundwork for this moment, here in Australia and around the world.

* * *

Decades before Mostyn spoke, feminists began making inroads in policy and economics circles towards the recognition of the value of women's unpaid and paid care work. This work was initially described as 'reproductive labour', i.e. the child-care, elder care, cooking, cleaning, shopping and domestic logistics (now more popularly known as the 'mental load'). Basically, all the work that women do unpaid in their own home or for little pay in other people's homes or care settings.

The Italian Marxist feminist Silvia Federici first advanced the argument when she founded the Wages for Housework movement in 1972. Influenced by another Italian feminist, Mariarosa Dalla Costa, and the American activist Selma James, who argued that by working without pay in the home women were producing the labour force that capitalism exploited for profit, Federici founded the American chapter of Wages for Housework and wrote her own foundational essay in 1975, *Wages Against Housework*.

'To say that we want wages for housework is to expose the fact that housework is already money for capital, that capital has made and makes money out of cooking, smiling, and fucking,' wrote Federici. 'At the same time, it shows that we have cooked, smiled, and fucked throughout the years, not because it was easier for us than for anybody else, but because we did not have any other choice. Our faces have become distorted from so much smiling.'[34]

In response to the argument that women should do this work for free as 'labourers of love' because they were just naturally better suited to care work, Federici was scathing. It was not 'natural' for care to be the soul preserve of one gender, she argued, nor was it natural for some to be subjugated by an economic system that benefited a few; they were merely conventions of an all-encompassing economic system that had become so dominant we could scarcely imagine an alternative.

In 1988, the New Zealand economist Marilyn Waring took up the cause and published her ground-breaking book, *Counting for Nothing: What Men Value and What Women Are Worth*. The book explored how mainstream economics and the systems on which modern calculations of gross domestic product are based (the universal measure of a nation's economic wellbeing) exclude and make invisible women's contribution through 'life-sustaining' unpaid labour – that 'reproductive labour' Federici and her generation wrote about.

Waring had been appointed chair of the New Zealand government's Public Expenditure Committee in 1978. This experience opened her eyes to how invisible and marginal women's experiences were in the policy process, even though as 50 per cent of the population they were profoundly affected by the spending decisions the powerful Committee took. Waring demanded access to information from every government department about the gendered impacts of spending decisions. She also asked a Treasury official to explain why GDP excluded women's unpaid work. The answer: GDP formulations were based on the United Nations' System of National Accounts.

'Right, I want to see the rules,' Waring said, according to a 2018 profile in *The Monthly*. But it turned out there wasn't a copy of the UN's National Accounts in New Zealand, or Australia for that matter. 'So all these nations are using the United Nations System of National Accounts, these rules that run the whole of the data that everyone uses, without anyone having read them … That's what we call propaganda,' Waring told *The Monthly*.

Waring later travelled to New York to research the System of National Accounts. A soul-destroying moment occurred when she read a 1953 edition that casually dismissed women's unpaid labour as 'of little or no importance'. GDP, in excluding the unpaid labour of one gender, is based on 'an ideology of applied patriarchy', she told *The Monthly*. As Anne Manne reflected in the piece, 'Human activities of great value are made invisible, treated as meaningless.'[35]

Though the System of National Accounts was revised in 1993 and again in 2008 as a result of Waring's work, the exclusion of women's unpaid work remained consistent, though the National Accounts made a provision for a separate but consistent set of satellite accounts that gave value to women's unpaid work but always sat alongside GDP.

The monetary value of unpaid care work in Australia has been estimated to be $650.1 billion, equivalent to 50.6 per cent of GDP.[36] This makes it Australia's largest industry, larger than any in the formal economy.[37] That's the equivalent of the value of three mining industries.

Other economists, like the US-based Nancy Folbre, a professor emerita of economics at the University of Massachusetts Amherst Political Economy Research Institute, have also devoted their life's work to this issue. In 1998, Folbre received a MacArthur Genius Grant for her work exploring how the care sector, defined as activity in the home and the market, was a crucial part of the economy but operated differently to other parts of the economy. Folbre argues that the economic productivity and incentives of child care centres are incomparable to other industries in that the 'profits' are shared by the child care centre, the children, their parents, and wider society.[38]

Nearly two decades after Folbre was awarded that Genius Grant, the term 'infrastructure' in reference to care-related work was first used by Ai-jen Poo, an American labour activist and director of the National Domestic Workers Alliance, in her 2015 book, *The Age of Dignity: Preparing for the Elder Boom in a Changing America*.[39]

'If we can deliver water and electricity and internet to every home in this country, we should be able to create good care options for everyone,' Poo said in a recent interview.

Described as a 'wake-up call about the demographic reality that will affect us all' and a book that 'demonstrates the interconnectedness of elder care issues with the rights of women, immigrants, and all workers', *The Age of Dignity* sets out a roadmap for how America could become a more caring nation, provide solutions for fixing the fraying care sector *and* provide opportunities for women, immigrants and the unemployed. A bestseller, Poo's book put the idea of care and care feminism on the contemporary feminist agenda. 'Care is the strategy and the solution toward a better future for all of us,' she proclaimed.

By 2019, those who had long sounded the alarm about the ticking time bomb of care were being taken seriously. The care economy was on the agenda of the four female senators who ran for the US presidency, bringing attention to the issue even before the pandemic threw it into even sharper relief.

In 2020, the newly elected Biden administration wove care as 'infrastructure' firmly into its pandemic recovery plans. President Biden included money for home-based care for the elderly and the disabled under the umbrella of infrastructure, as part of a $2 trillion package he proposed in March. The next month, he proposed more funding for paid family leave, universal early years education and care, and $225 billion for childcare. And in May, business leaders lent their support to the cause when Time's Up launched the Care Economy

Business Council, a coalition of nearly 200 businesses across industries with a mission to reimagine the nation's caregiving infrastructure so people could get back to work and build a stronger, more resilient economy. Governments and industries could now see the need to actively invest in care industries and ergo valued them more highly, seeing them as an essential part of the economy and not just some adjunct that women do because they love it.

Here in Australia, Elizabeth Hill, an associate professor of political economy at the University of Sydney and co-convenor of the Australian Work + Family Policy Roundtable, has been foundational to this shift.

'It is absolutely extraordinary that we've got to this place,' Hill told me. 'We used to be a voice in the wilderness, and now we have so many friends and colleagues of all persuasions making the kinds of arguments that we've been making for a really long time. And making them in powerful ways and from really powerful platforms.'

'It is edifying,' added Hill. 'See, we were right all along.'

I could, however, recall a time in recent memory when this was most certainly not the case, and the dire warnings of what would happen – and actually did happen – if we failed to change tack.

* * *

When I was working at the UK's Equal Opportunity Commission (EOC) more than a decade ago, a policy officer came to me with a paper on the undervaluing of women's work. I was the head of media at the time, and she was hoping I could get a bit of press for this beige-sounding but vitally important feminist issue. The undervaluing of women's work accounts for about one-fifth of the gender pay gap in Australia, but it is rarely talked about outside of the most earnest of policy circles. The situation in the UK at the time was broadly similar. The EOC paper warned that the undervaluing of women's work was contributing to 'a caring time bomb'. Those words, and that stark warning, have stayed with me ever since.

The undervaluing of women's work is essentially the fact that female-dominated industries are valued less than male-dominated industries *simply because the work is done by women.* Working in a female-dominated occupation can reduce pay by as much as 9 per cent. Nowhere is that clearer than in the caring professions, where we have – for too long – expected women to work for poverty wages as 'labourers of love'. The tragic consequences of that became visible in the course of the pandemic, as each and every day our aged care homes, early years sector, disability sector and nursing struggled to cope. We had reached the end of the fuse on that 'caring time bomb' that the EOC paper had warned about more than a decade before. And the impacts have been horrific.

In aged care, a 2021 report warned that poor pay, stress and excessive paperwork had pushed Australia to the precipice of an aged care staffing crisis. The report warned of a 'mass exodus', with 65 per cent of workers intending to leave the residential aged care industry within the next five years.[40]

By the summer of 2022 – in the midst of the Omicron wave – those dire predictions had come true. Against a backdrop of more aged care residents dying of COVID-19 in January 2022 than in the whole of the previous year, and shocking reports of neglect due to understaffing (lack of meals, showers, etc.), unions and industry groups jointly appealed to the federal government for help to resolve the increasingly desperate staffing shortages. The clearest sign of that desperation: a call for the federal government to deploy the military to residential aged care homes.

Over in the childcare sector, the January 2022 Omicron wave was also taking its toll. Four hundred and twenty childcare centres had closed across Australia due to COVID-19, and more were warning they would have to close due to staff shortages and reduced attendance. By February 2022, the federal government was being urged to inject $1 billion into the sector to fix the crisis. More than one in eight childcare centres had waivers from the sector's quality regulator to allow them to operate for at least twelve months without meeting legal staffing requirements. Personally, as a parent of two children, I daren't let my mind entertain the possibilities of what understaffed childcare centres might lead to. It's too distressing.

And in the healthcare sector, where 75 per cent of the workforce is female, thousands of fed-up nurses took to the streets in New South Wales in February 2022 for the first strike in more than a decade to demand better pay and conditions. Such was the strength of feeling, they marched in defiance of orders from the Industrial Relations Commission to call the action off. Keep your 'claps for carers', was their message. We need more than that.

As Mostyn suggested in her speech at the National Press Club, Australia was indeed a 'lucky country' to have availed itself of these women's good will to work for so little or no pay. But Australia's luck, it was clear, was now running out.

People across Australia could connect the undervaluing of women's care work to their own lives, to the lives of their elderly relatives, to the lives of their children, to the lives of their disabled friends and family in a real way that they, perhaps, couldn't before.

A clear sign of this shift and new momentum towards care feminism: the unlikely coalition of Women for Progress in early 2022, a group of prominent women from diverse backgrounds and experiences whose aim was to highlight the role of women and girls in the COVID-19 recovery as a critical policy issue for government. The group ranged in membership from an icon of the Australian women's movement, Wendy McCarthy, and former foreign minister Julie Bishop to ACTU president Michele O'Neil, Aboriginal and Torres Strait Islander Social Justice commissioner June Oscar and Diversity Council of Australia chair Ming Long. It also, notably, included Sam Mostyn.

Among their calls to action was advocating for an unprecedented investment in Australia's caring infrastructure, including greater investment in early years education and the proper remuneration of the people (mostly women) who did vital, dare we say essential, care work.

By early 2022, the movement from career feminism to care feminism was well advanced. And long overdue. It goes without saying that an army of carers, paid and unpaid, should not have been forced to pay such a high price in the course of the pandemic in terms of their wellbeing and mental health to help prompt this reappraisal, but we have arrived at a very different place. This has set us up brilliantly to reassess some of the issues so vital to a new deal for women at work that have not been at the top of the lean-in agenda.

# 3.

# BURNOUT, PANDEMIC STYLE

Dr Nisha Khot, a Melbourne-based obstetrician and the mother of two children aged twelve and eighteen, said it crept up on her. When the pandemic first arrived on Australian shores in March 2020, she thought to herself, 'Our kids are older, we'll be okay.' Then it slowly dawned on her that everything wasn't going to be okay.

As an essential worker, Khot said that she struggled to keep up with the demands of her job, especially as many of her colleagues fell victim to the virus or, like her, contended with the demands of work and caring for children. Many of her colleagues had younger children and – Khot felt – their need for flexibility was greater than hers. She took on more shifts, put her hand up to cover work or childcare or anything else she could do to help. 'I reached out to colleagues I felt were struggling, with phone calls, virtual coffee, DM on Twitter, anything I could do to help,' Khot said.

When Melbourne went back into lockdown in August 2021, this time with even more stringent Stage 4 restrictions – which meant the continuation of remote learning for children, but also a curfew and extremely limited movement of no more than 5 kilometres from home 'for work, food, supplies and caregiving' – something had to give. 'I have always been the one who does more of the parenting,' Khot told me. 'That time around, it was just too difficult; I found that I just wasn't interested.'

'Essentially, I gave up,' Khot said. For her, that meant becoming less connected and more inward looking. 'I functioned on autopilot. I didn't look forward to anything, I didn't enjoy anything. I stopped being present.'

Ashleigh Rodgers, a lawyer based on the Mornington Peninsula, near Melbourne, and the mother of a two-year-old daughter, also struggled when Victoria was plunged back into lockdown in 2021. She told me that the stress began at the start of the very first lockdown, in 2020, when she was faced with the 'difficult' decision to pull her daughter out of childcare. Rodgers was then presented with the new pandemic juggle of trying to get her own work done while caring for her daughter. Her partner, who worked in commercial construction as a site operator, was still required to leave the family home and be onsite for work.

'Juggling work and care, providing my daughter with activities, trying to do my job *and* make sure she was having relatively the same activities she would have had at day care, it was really hard,' Rodgers said. 'I experienced a heightened sense of anxiety, and physically I had moments when I was overwhelmed by it all,' she added. 'It's that uncertainty. I'm a very structured person. I struggled with the fact that not only was it an uncertain time for me and my husband, but it was uncertain for my daughter as well.'

Over in the female-dominated, traditionally undervalued industries (meaning poorly paid simply because the profession is dominated by women) thrust onto the pandemic front line overnight, Virginia Ellis is a fifty-five-year-old aged care worker who has worked in the sector for fifteen years. Based in the Blue Mountains just west of Sydney, Ellis told me that she regularly worked ten-hour shifts even before the pandemic. But as the sector struggled with the demands of repeated lockdowns and the overwhelming impact of the pandemic on people in their care, who were far more vulnerable to the virus, things only got worse. The days were long, but she 'loved' the job, she said. 'In my role I do everything. From the time I walk in at eight o'clock in the morning I'm non-stop until I finish at six in the evening,' she said. 'Sometimes I don't get a lunch break.'

'But a lot of people I work with struggle to make ends meet or pay the rent,' added Ellis. 'I see them picking up extra shifts to get by, and I often think to myself: with childcare and travelling to and fro, is it worth it? But I guess that extra little bit helps. But they're tired. They're exhausted.'

On $28 an hour, Ellis said that her work was grossly undervalued, and that sense of injustice – particularly in the context of the increased demands of the pandemic – only added to the fatigue: 'It's a very rewarding job, but it's not respected. You hear it all the time: "Well, you're just a carer."' It was this soul-destroying, grinding triple whammy of work stress, poor pay and the lack of respect, said Ellis, that drove a mental and physical health crisis for those in the caring sectors that the 'claps for carers' simply couldn't remedy.

The pandemic has given rise to numerous mental health challenges for women, including a particularly virulent strain of burnout that has disproportionately impacted women, especially mothers, women in the female-dominated frontline caring professions and women from diverse backgrounds. And the tail of this particular burnout crisis, according to experts, will be long. For these women, the mantras of Sandberg's nearly decade-old *Lean In* were of little use – and little comfort – in the face of a pandemic. And their experiences over the last two years have proven to many, some for the first time, just how useless those nostrums always were.

A 2022 report from Deloitte warned of the 'worrying longer-term impact' of this 'pandemic postscript of alarmingly high levels of burnout'. Half of all Australian women now, according to the report, say they feel burned out and more than half say their stress levels are *higher* than they were a year ago; 45 per cent say their mental health is extremely poor or poor, and 32 per cent are taking time off work due to mental health challenges.

Women also reported experiencing higher levels of so-called 'non-inclusive' behaviours in 2021 than 2020, and that these behaviours contributed to their overall lack of wellbeing. Meanwhile, women in ethnic minority groups, according to the report, were even more likely to experience those non-inclusive behaviours, with 25 per cent reporting someone else taking credit for their work, for example, compared to 9 per cent of the broader cohort.[41]

The Multicultural Centre for Women's Health and Gender Equity Victoria painted a devastating picture of the impacts of the pandemic on the mental health of migrant and refugee women in their *Left Behind* report. Migrant and refugee women were over-represented in essential services such as aged care, cleaning, retail and manufacturing and, as a result, at greater risk of COVID-19 infection. What's more, in many cases they were excluded from government support like JobKeeper due to their visa status, which contributed to distress and economic uncertainty. In-language interviews with seventy-five Victorian migrant women showed that COVID-19 decreased their economic and job security, their mental health and resilience, and their social and family ties.[42]

The way that we talk about women and work has shifted in the last two years from do-it-yourself lean-in mantras, to a broader conversation about the context in which women work and what needs to change. And nowhere is that more clear than in the conversation around workplace burnout.

The technical definition of clinical-level burnout is exhaustion, a sense of futility and difficulty maintaining personal connections. And even before the pandemic, there was always what's called a 'burnout gender gap', meaning women were more likely than men to experience burnout at work.

But the pandemic turbo-charged that gap: the size of the 'burnout gender gap' has more than doubled since 2019, according to a 2021 Gallup poll: 34 per cent of American women now feel burned out at work compared to 26 per cent of men.[43]

What's more, there has always been a sizeable 'power gap' in terms of which women are more likely to experience that burnout. It's not the women in the boardroom, according to the Gallup poll, but the women in non-leadership roles who have less agency or control over their working lives, and, perhaps, more of an acute sense of injustice about their pay, conditions, and the discrimination (gender, race, disability, sexual orientation, gender identity) they face.

And it's the women with children, particularly young children, who have less control over their time, and struggle to balance the demands of work and home life. We all know that while women have entered the workforce in large numbers over the last four decades, they still – in Australia and around the world – carry a larger share of the unpaid domestic burden. During the pandemic that load only increased.

And, finally, in addition to the 'burnout gender gap' and 'burnout power gap', there has also always been an 'ethnic minority burnout gap', with women of colour and Aboriginal and Torres Strait Islander women more likely to experience it than white women. And this, too, has been exacerbated by the pandemic. A 2019 survey of Harvard Business School graduates found that while 17 per cent of respondents said that they 'often' or 'very often' experienced burnout at work and 23 per cent of women said they did, that rose to 30 per cent for women of colour.[44] The reason: the additional layer of racism and microaggressions women of colour experience at work.

In Australia, a 2021 report from the Workplace Gender Equality Agency, in partnership with the Jumbunna Institute for Indigenous Education and Research, and Diversity Council Australia, found that Aboriginal and Torres Strait Islander women had significantly less support in culturally unsafe situations and they carried the highest cultural load.[45] For those unfamiliar with the concept of 'cultural load', it refers to the (unpaid) expectation that someone should make the workplace more culturally inclusive. Three in five Indigenous women in management reported that they experienced 'moderate' or 'high' expectations to carry that load, according to the study.

Another Australian survey focused on women of colour found that almost 60 per cent of respondents experienced discrimination in the workplace,[46] while a 2017 report showed that 'only 1 in 5 culturally diverse women in Australia felt their workplace was free of cultural diversity- or gender-based biases and stereotypes'.[47] And research has shown that women with disability face higher rates of sexual harassment, violence, abuse and discrimination in the workplace than women without disability.[48]

'[The pandemic has] been absolute hell in terms of women's mental health,' Professor Jayashri Kulkarni, a professor of psychiatry at Alfred Health and Monash University, told me when asked to describe the trends she has observed over the course of the pandemic in terms of women's mental health. 'The increase in anxiety disorders, depression disorders, alcohol use disorders, eating disorders, they have all really escalated in women – and that's across the globe; and even when the infection and financial aspects of the crisis are more under control, this is going to be something that really hurts for quite some time.'

'It's as if women started from a further back position, because already women were experiencing about a four-to-one female-to-male ratio for anxiety and two-to-one depression,' she added. 'And then you add the burden of the financial stability, the loss of their jobs as women were over-represented in the casual workforce … But, also, other things that we didn't expect: the impact of the anxieties about catching the virus for the healthcare workers, who are largely female on the front line, was significant. Nursing staff, clerical staff, cleaning staff, aged care staff and so on, these are all very female-dominated workforces. The levels of anxiety sky-rocketed because of the fear of the infection, but also due to the rapid changes in the ways their work was done.'

For working mothers, the pandemic also brought an extra level of stress. Dr Pooja Lakshmin is a US-based psychiatrist and author who also specialises in women's mental health with a focus on how broken social systems impact women's emotional lives. In a 2021 article for *The New York Times*, she suggested an alternative to the use of the word 'burnout': 'this isn't just about burnout, it's about betrayal', read the subhead of Lakshmin's article.[49]

'The more I hear my patients use the term "burnout," the more I think it doesn't capture the depth of despair they describe,' wrote Lakshmin. 'These are mothers who are faced with impossible choices: sending their child to school, and risking viral exposure, or not showing up to work; plopping their child down in front of a screen just to get a moment of peace.'

Likening what mothers experienced to the kind of 'moral injury' frequently experienced by physicians (moral injury is the concept that systemic problems in the medical industry prevent doctors from doing what they know is right for their patients), Lakshmin wrote that the crushing toll on working mothers' mental health, in particular, reflected that level of societal 'betrayal'. 'While burnout places the blame (and thus the responsibility) on the individual and tells working moms they aren't resilient enough, betrayal points directly to the broken structures around them,' she wrote.

Here in Australia, others noted similar patterns and sought to find a word or phrase that could adequately capture the true scale of what women were experiencing. Professor Leisa Sargent, the senior deputy dean of UNSW Business School and the university's co-deputy vice-chancellor Equity, Diversity and Inclusion, opted for the 'Great Exhaustion', a play on the so-called 'Great Resignation' in the United States that has seen women exit the workforce in far greater numbers than men. For Sargent, the 'Great Exhaustion' is defined as 'the absolute overwhelming feeling of emotional exhaustion like there's "nothing left in the tank"'.[50]

'Betrayal' and 'nothing left in the tank'. Yes, we might be starting to capture the true depths of what many women have experienced these past two years, how it's impacting on their desire and capacity to work in the years ahead, and how it's changing the conversation around burnout, arguably for the better.

All this comes at a cost. Employees who often or always feel burned out at work are 63 per cent more likely to take a sick day and 2.6 times more likely to leave their employer.[51] And that was before the pandemic. Now there's solid evidence that the last two years have affected women's ambition and satisfaction at work, potentially fuelling a mass exodus from the workplace.

A 2021 US study found that four in ten women in the corporate world were thinking of leaving their company or switching jobs. And women in the US have already exited the labour force at twice the rate of men. Their participation in the paid labour force is now the lowest it has been in more than thirty years; about one-third of all mothers in the workforce have scaled back or left their jobs since March 2020.[52]

In Australia, women's workforce participation is currently at a historically high level post lockdown. But there are serious risks to the 'pandemic postscript' of burnout, as Deloitte Australia put it, and the risk remains that Australian women could likewise pursue a Great Resignation with devasting consequences for their own long-term economic security, as well as Australia's broader productivity. Australian employers are already struggling to find staff to fill vacancies, and tapping into Australia's highly educated female workforce could help.

The 2021 *Women's Agenda Women's Ambition Report* found that 39 per cent of women said burnout might get in the way of their ambition over the next two years, and 28 per cent felt less optimistic about their career prospects.[53] And according to the Australian results of Deloitte's 2021 *Women @ Work* survey, a majority of Australian women surveyed said they felt less optimistic about their career prospects than before the pandemic, and nearly a quarter said they might leave the workforce for good.[54]

That's one in four pondering leaving the workforce … *for good.*

If that happens, warns Steve Hatfield, Deloitte's global leader for Future of Work, there's a danger that this could translate into a lack of working women role models, particularly mothers and diverse women – with long-lasting consequences. As the saying goes, 'You can't be what you can't see.'

* * *

How do we begin to tackle the Great Exhaustion? Part of the answer lies in changing the conversation. We need to move away from lean-in ideas that posit the solution rests with individual women alone, who should devote more time and energy to their 'wellbeing' and simply shore up their resilience. Beware corporate 'feminist wellness', selling a soothing balm of herbal tea and scented candles – faux feminist Prozac to help women recover from the uniquely gendered impacts of the pandemic – instead of structural change.

Many are fond of quoting the late activist Audre Lorde, who once wrote, 'Caring for myself is not self-indulgence, it is self-preservation, and that is an act of political warfare.' And while that is absolutely true – and they are wise words for a growing army of feminist activists who are now taking to the streets in pursuit of gender equality – self-care as an idea and now an industry has been twisted beyond all recognition from Lorde's original meaning.

This is 'feminist wellness' or self-care as a kind of escape, not, as Lorde intended, a restorative practice to give those seeking deeper, collective change the energy and resilience to persevere. This kind of feminist self-care is, at best, devoid of meaning in its attempt to move product or, at worst, a cynical attempt to divert women from the task at hand.

No one ever said, 'Nevertheless she persisted with her daily regime of scented candles and massage therapy.' (Though if I close my eyes and listen, I can almost imagine Gwyneth Paltrow uttering those words.)

The rise of the wellness industrial complex, particularly in relation to women, is mirrored by the way neoliberalism infected feminism in the 1990s. No structural inequalities to tackle collectively here, folks. This is an individual problem. But as Angela Priestley, the founding editor of *Women's Agenda,* told me, 'this isn't something more lunchtime pilates will fix'.

This is *not* what we need at this critical juncture.

'It's really important that we look at the higher-level factors that have led to all of this,' Dr Adele Murdolo, the executive director of Australia's Multicultural Centre for Women's Health, told me. COVID caused lots of stuff, but it also just exacerbated a lot of inequality that was already there. It showed it up and it made it more apparent to everybody.

'We need to have a look at gender and race discrimination in the workplace and develop policies and programs that are knocking that off at the source, which is a big job and not something you can fix in a month because it's something that's so embedded in our workplaces,' added Murdolo.

Lisa Annese, CEO of Diversity Council Australia, has said that 'inclusion at work is an antidote to the great resignation'. She points to new research from DCA that demonstrates the link between non-inclusive behaviours and workers' intentions to stay. Workers in inclusive teams are 4 times more likely than those in non-inclusive teams to report their workplace has positively impacted their mental health, and they are 4 times less likely to leave their jobs. 'So you are investing in the wellbeing of your people, and making your business more resilient.'[55]

We need to develop policies, legislation and programs that change not only workplace cultures and attitudes, but also the way that workplaces are structured; at the moment, workforces are really about the full-time, unencumbered male employee. We need to look at making workplaces really flexible. Not flexible just for employers in terms of insecure work, but flexible for what people in families really need. We need childcare so that women are able to actively participate in the workforce. We need to tackle the gender pay gap, and not just as it relates to gender alone, but also taking into account ethnicity, disability and sexual orientation ... all the intersecting forms of discrimination that make the gender pay gap even larger for some than others (more on this in Chapter 4).

'Bigger structural issues: pay equity, equal jobs of equal worth (particularly for women in undervalued caring jobs), childcare, giving people permission to voice the good, bad and the ugly is also part of the healing process,' Leisa Sargent told me. 'But I also think that making sure that employees are engaged in the decision-making process coming out of the pandemic is really important. We went through two years of being told what we had to do and how we had to do it, which is very disempowering.'

We now need to create opportunities where people feel they have a say in how things get done, in flexibility, in opportunities to work in different parts of the business and to be stimulated.

'And it's also about a fundamental redrawing of the boundaries,' added Sargent.

Research from the Australia Institute's Centre for Future Work suggests why a redrawing of boundaries may be particularly necessary, as the pandemic has only exacerbated the trend towards the intensification of work and highlighted the costs of insecure work, where women are heavily concentrated. The research found that the average worker did 6.1 hours per week of unpaid overtime in 2021, a substantial increase on 2020.[56]

'Let's make jobs plentiful, safer, secure and invest in social institutions that support people, in particular women, to work', Alison Pennington, a senior economist at the Centre for Future Work, told me was the quite simple, yet powerful, prescription. 'The treadmill of insecure work fuels anxiety and makes planning for a decent life nigh impossible. The reality is that the human cost of unchecked employer power is enormous. And there are multiple indicators that this power has deepened over the pandemic.'

The solutions are structural and collective, going far beyond self-care, and even beyond direct psychological treatment for women's mental health, though this is undeniably necessary and should be addressed with more targeted and innovative mental health support. At the time we spoke, Professor Jayashri Kulkarni, for example, had just opened Australia's first dedicated mental health centre for women, a specialist model she would like to see replicated elsewhere.

As we endeavour to 'build back better', we need these types of broad, wide-ranging proposals as part of the wider debate about women and work. The changed conversation around women's workplace burnout and the factors driving that will play a significant role in moving the conversation forward from the lean-in feminism that has so far dominated the Australian landscape to something better, something more impactful and meaningful. If that happens, then women's collective suffering during the pandemic won't have been in vain.

# 4.

# 'KNOW YOUR WORTH': THE GENDER PAY GAP'S BIG LIE

In 1969, Zelda D'Aprano chained herself to the doors of the Melbourne Commonwealth Building to protest the limited nature of the outcome of an equal pay case in which she was a party, along with other women from the Australasian Meat Industry Employees' Union (AMIEU).

'No more male and female rates, one rate only' read her now-famous sign. It beggars belief, but this was quite a revolutionary idea at a time when it was perfectly legal to pay men and women differently for doing … the exact same job.

Though D'Aprano was eventually cut free by police, ten days later she was back, this time with two friends, Alva Geikie and Thelma Solomon. They chained themselves to the doors of the Arbitration Court, which had dismissed their claim to equal pay.

Born in 1928 in Melbourne to European immigrants, D'Aprano left school at fourteen to work in a variety of factory jobs before gaining qualifications as a dental nurse.

She later worked as a clerk for the AMIEU and also as a mail sorter. It's fair to say that D'Aprano's militancy in the workplace resulted in her being fired from more than one job. The personal consequences, however, never seemed to deter her.

A year after D'Aprano chained herself to the doors of the Commonwealth Building, she, along with Geikie and Solomon, founded the Women's Action Committee and the Women's Liberation Centre, from which the Women's Liberation Movement in Melbourne was born. The Committee sought to get women more involved in collective activism, shedding the metaphorical chains of a culture requiring them to be 'ladylike' and 'polite' in their quest for change, which D'Aprano had quickly recognised would never result in a revolution.

D'Aprano and her fellow activists travelled around Melbourne by public transport paying only 75 per cent of the fares because women were only given 75 per cent of the wage of men at the time. They did pub crawls, because women weren't allowed to drink in bars, only in lounges. And they helped arrange the first pro-choice rally in 1975.

The case that prompted D'Aprano's protest was brought by the AMIEU and other workers' groups to the Commonwealth Conciliation and Arbitration Commission, and it argued for equal pay for all employees. Instead, the Commission's ruling established a general female award minimum wage of 85 per cent of the male wage, in recognition of the fact that men were 'breadwinners' who should be paid more because they had families to support.

In 1972, the Commission revisited that decision and ruled that women and men undertaking similar work that had similar value were eligible for the same rate. And in 1973 a ruling by the Commission granted an equal minimum wage to all Australians, regardless of their sex. Finally, in 1974, the 'breadwinner' component of a male wage was removed, an acknowledgement that more Australian women were providing for their families.[57]

As Mary Gaudron, a lawyer and judge who was the first female justice of the High Court of Australia, once said, 'We got equal pay once. Then we got it again. Then we got it again, and we still don't have it.'

Today, fifty years after that ruling establishing equal pay for work of equal value, there's still a gender pay gap in Australia of 13.8 per cent. This means that the average Australian woman still has to work an extra sixty-one days a year to earn the same pay as a man.[58] And while it fluctuates slightly up or down from year to year, the rate of change is, overall, painfully slow.

Before the pandemic, the Workplace Gender Equality Agency calculated that at the current rate of change, the gap would take until around 2050 to close.[59] After the pandemic arrived, many experts warned that the impacts could set us back a generation or more in terms of closing the gender pay gap. In May 2020, Kate Jenkins, Australia's sex discrimination commissioner, sounded the alarm, saying 'this is laying the groundwork for some pretty serious poverty for women'.[60]

And for some women in the traditionally undervalued, female-dominated caring professions, the gender pay gap, according to research from Bankwest Curtin Economics, will probably never close. Never!

That's pretty sobering when you consider that the same research found that the gender pay gap among full-time executives could be eliminated within ten years, and for senior managers in less than fifteen years. 'But for workers in non-management roles, it could take even longer,' cautioned Bankwest's deputy director, Associate Professor Rebecca Cassells. 'And some occupations [undervalued, female-dominated professions] may not see any change at all in their gender pay gap.'[61]

The reasons the gender pay gap has never fully closed are complicated, and it's important to note that it's not exclusively due to men and women being paid differently for doing the exact same job, as D'Aprano, rightly, protested all those years ago. But they are all unjust.

This is, clearly, unfinished business. And as the pandemic has shown us just how fragile progress has been for women in the workplace, it's a reminder to all of us to maintain focus ... and rage. I fervently hope that we'll see a new push to close the gender pay gap in 2022, the fiftieth anniversary of that first major milestone of progress in 1972. And I hope that – after what women have been through these past two-plus years – it will be very much in the spirit of Zelda, not Sheryl Sandberg.

* * *

There's a beautiful thing about the gender pay gap (and, yes, I know it feels a bit wrong to say there is something 'beautiful' about a figure that represents women earning, on average, $255.30 less per week than men): it's a composite figure that represents the myriad of injustices that women experience in the workplace. These injustices range from gender and intersecting forms of race and disability discrimination, to the unequal distribution of caring responsibilities at home, to the cost of childcare, to the fact that we don't properly value the paid and unpaid care work that women do.

What are the drivers of the gender pay gap? According to a 2019 report from the Diversity Council of Australia and the Workplace Gender Equality Agency, the top three drivers are gender discrimination (39 per cent), years not working or career interruptions due to caring responsibilities (25 per cent), and the undervaluing of women's work that comes from what's called industry and occupational segregation (17 per cent). Disturbingly, the report found that gender discrimination – the single largest factor – was on the increase, as was the impact of the second biggest driver, caring responsibilities.[62]

As Mary Gaudron put it, we got equal pay again and again, but 'we still don't have it'.

Why the lack of progress – indeed, the backwards slide? I suspect one factor is lean-in feminism and its giant 'Hey, look over here' distraction about women's inability to ask for more money. For example, in 2007, a book called *Women Don't Ask* made a big splash, claiming that women, unlike men, don't negotiate over pay and, as a result, they are paid less. Sandberg's *Lean In* offered a similar theory.

Women should just ask for more money! Problem solved!

Unfortunately, we would have to wait more than ten years for this load of nonsense to be thoroughly debunked. A 2018 study, 'Do Women Ask?', found that women do ask just as much as men; they just don't get what they ask for. The researchers examined 4600 Australian employees from 800 workplaces and found that 'the patterns we found are consistent with the idea that women's requests for advancement are treated differently from men's requests. Asking does not mean getting, at least if you are female'.[63]

What's more, the now well-established theory of 'gender backlash' also undermines the efficacy of this 'solution' to pay equity. Let's just call it the Henry Higgins theory of inclusion and diversity: 'Why can't a woman be more like a man?' On the one hand, lots of research shows that society tends to associate stereotypically male attributes with those of an effective leader. So, the logic follows, to succeed as a leader a woman should simply adopt stereotypically male traits, including acting more 'assertively'.

But here's the problem: research also tells us that women who do act more assertively, behaving in a stereotypically male way, are seen to be breaching feminine norms and suffer a penalty.[64] Asking for a promotion, offering unsolicited opinions, challenging the status quo, speaking up about concerns or negotiating for that pay rise may help men get ahead, but women are labelled as 'bossy' (or worse) for the exact same behaviour – and they pay a price.

In a 2008 study published in *Psychological Science*, men received a boost in their perceived status after expressing anger. In contrast, 'women who expressed anger were consistently accorded lower status and lower wages, and were seen as less competent'.[65] Another study showed that when men and women were equally aggressive in the workplace, women's 'perceived deserved compensation' dropped by 35 per cent, twice as much as men's.[66]

Any readers to whom this may apply should contact the 'salary negotiation skills for women' training provider they once forked out some cash to and ask for a refund. A quick Google search yields dozens of such lean-in purveyors still peddling this nonsense. One course even lasts three weeks. That's a long time to spend listening to someone, possibly a woman in a white blazer with gold buttons, telling you that you're the problem.

Lean-in feminists took this inconvenient truth in their stride and came up with another faux solution: 'gender judo'. As Joan C. Williams and Rachel Dempsey co-wrote in their 2014 book *What Works for Women at Work*, powerful women should take feminine stereotypes that can hold women back – the selfless mother and the dutiful daughter, for example – and use them to propel themselves forward.[67] Women could now tie themselves into knots trying to find just the right balance of sugar, spice and everything nice that men wouldn't find threatening.

And that's how we ended up with women on leadership-type websites offering tips like this: 'Use a brief framing statement like: "I know it's a risk for women to speak this assertively, but I'm going to express my opinion very directly"'. Or 'to adopt dominant body language and direct speech but keep messages communal' while also 'simultaneously communicating competence and warmth'. Yes, this had all become very, very silly.

These convoluted 'solutions' reflect the belief of some – with varying degrees of good intentions – that we should engage with the world as it is, rather than the world as we would like it to be.

But, as is ever the case – and really the point of this book – individual solutions are not going to be the answer. While one woman might be transformed from a 'nice girl who doesn't ask' to a 'bold woman taking control of her career who knows her worth', her individual success in the sense that *she* makes more money does nothing to tackle the broader structural drivers of the gender pay gap.

It's time we started engaging in, and fighting for, the world as we would like it to be, and to look again at the big, bold, structural solutions that tackle the real drivers of the gender pay gap.

Fortunately for Australia, we are poised for another big, effective push to close the remaining gender pay gap, and it's pretty clear what needs to happen now. This includes action to make childcare more affordable and accessible, parental leave equality to help level the domestic playing field for women at home, increased wages and conditions for the many women working in female-dominated caring industries such as aged care, and action to tackle the various forms of gender, race, disability, sexual orientation and gender identity discrimination that drive women out of the workplace, including sexual harassment and pregnancy discrimination, all the kinds discussed in this book.

But the first big necessary step is increased transparency.

In 2021, the Australian branch of the Global Institute of Women's Leadership (GIWL) and the Australian National University published a report that highlighted how Australia had lost its way in terms of gender pay transparency, *Gender Pay Gap Reporting in Australia: Time for an Upgrade*.

The report noted the need for a 'multifaceted approach' that tackled improved parental leave, particularly for men, affordable childcare and the valuing of work stereotypically done by women. But the report also noted the critical need to increase 'pay transparency' – so that employees know the size of the gender pay gap at their particular place of employment and can, presumably, feel empowered to do something about it.

The report noted that Australia compared poorly with other nations on gender equality reporting. 'Australia received the joint-lowest ranking on the gender pay gap reporting scorecard across all countries studied,' concluded the study's authors.[68]

A particular issue identified in the report was the lack of public disclosure. The Workplace Gender Equality Agency currently publishes the size of the gender pay gap as a national and industry composite, but doesn't publish the size of the gender pay gap at individual employers. Individual employer reporting has been the law in the UK, for example, since 2017.

The GIWL study authors somewhat euphemistically described the problem as such: 'the absence of qualitative data or action plan disclosure impedes stakeholders' ability to engage with individual employers about their gender equality activities'. Let me translate that into plain English: without knowing the size of the gender pay gap at their place of employment, women can't stick their head above the parapet, lock eyes with their colleagues and say, collectively, 'What the fuck is going on here?'

The GIWL report also highlighted a lack of 'intersectional data' – such as Indigenous status, disability and cultural background – which means 'it is difficult to understand how gender intersects with other factors'. Translation: this makes it difficult for diverse groups of women to highlight why they have every right to be mightily pissed off about how little they make compared to white women and men.

In that regard, consider this: Australia and the US both have an annual Equal Pay Day to rally activists to close the gender pay gap, each event held on a date that symbolises the additional days a woman must work, on average, to earn the same amount as a man. But the US also has a Black Women's

Equal Pay Day, held on a date that marks the additional days Black women need to work to catch up to white men *and* white women. We simply can't do that here in Australia until we collect and publish the intersectional data.

As I said, if there's something beautiful about the gender pay gap, it's that it highlights the many injustices women experience in the workplace; so too it should highlight the intersecting forms of injustice experienced by women from diverse backgrounds. The fact that we still don't collect and publish this data is likely a reflection of the dominant strain of lean-in feminism, which is indifferent to these issues.

Fortunately, and somewhat miraculously, a review into the *Workplace Gender Equality Act* published by the Department of the Prime Minister and Cabinet in March 2022 recommended that these reporting omissions be rectified: there should be mandatory public gender pay gap reporting for individual employers, and intersectional gender pay gap data should be collected and published.[69] Perhaps recognising the radical implications of these changes, the Morrison government responded by saying that they were 'working towards' the implementation pending 'further consultation with business'.

But change is afoot. The new Labor government under Prime Minister Anthony Albanese has promised to implement the recommendations of the review in full. That would be a big step towards changing workplace culture, and, along with reforms such as structural changes in childcare, parental leave reforms, and the proper valuing of women's work, could push us that little bit further towards tackling gender inequality. And maybe we can finally consign all those negotiation tips and gender judo to the dustbin of equal pay history.

# 5.
# THE HOME FRONT

In May 2020, shortly after the world was plunged into the first COVID-19 lockdown, I went on ABC TV to talk about one of my favourite bugbears: domestic democracy. Or, more precisely, our lack thereof.

Even before COVID-19, Australian women did 2.3 more hours of unpaid domestic labour per day than men.[70] And according to a 2017 Oxfam analysis, 'Why the majority of the world's poor are women', women around the world do between two and ten times as much care and domestic work as men; the global value of that work is $10 trillion.[71] That's why, as the title of Oxfam's analysis of the report suggests, this gap – what many call the 'chores gap' – is a key driver of deeply entrenched feminised poverty in Australia and around the world; it pushes women, particularly women with children, out of paid work or onto the 'mummy track' of part-time work with poor pay and poor prospects.

Long before the pandemic, resentment about this uneven distribution of unpaid care and domestic work between men and women in heterosexual couples, particularly those with children, had been bubbling away beneath the surface. In response to that frustration, I once mused that perhaps the so-called 'chore wars', a long series of skirmishes on the feminist front line (or in pretty much any average, heterosexual household with kids) was about to go nuclear. There was evidence in the years preceding the pandemic that it could boil over, culminating in a series of viral essays[72] and best-selling books that gave voice to women's growing frustration. There was *All the Rage: Mothers, Fathers, and the Myth of Equal Partnership* by Darcy Lockman; *Fed Up: Emotional Labor, Women, and the Way Forward* by Gemma Hartley; *Fair Play: A Game-Changing Solution for When You Have Too Much to Do* by Eve Rodsky; and *The Home Stretch: Why it's Time to Come Clean About Who Does the Dishes* by Sally Howard.

And then the pandemic hit.

As we all took to our homes, I chirped on cheerfully to the ABC about how the lockdown experience could make all that so-called 'invisible' work women do in the home visible – maybe it's invisible because of that theory men don't 'see' the washing, or the laundry or maybe even the children, I mused, only half-jokingly.

Locked in our homes, how could men not lift their game? The experience could be potentially life changing, I suggested. 'For some families, men will have their eyes opened and they might prove more willing to take up the slack,' I said. I also expressed hope that – as we transitioned to working from home and the sky didn't fall in – perhaps both men *and* women might henceforth enjoy more flexibility at work well into the future, and this could help level the domestic playing field.[73]

Ah, to have such optimism.

In my defence, I wasn't alone in hoping that the pandemic might bring about a new reckoning in the eternal chore wars. A March 2020 research paper predicted that the historic pandemic moment would forever shift dynamics in families, leading to greater gender equality down the road.[74] If the #MeToo movement was a reckoning, prompting us to 'believe women', challenge men's privilege in the workplace, and re-evaluate our cultural tendency to discredit and sideline women's inconvenient stories of abuse, I wondered whether we were working up to a breakthrough in regard to the barely shifting unequal distribution of work at home.

Again, who was this Pollyanna on steroids?

Within a few months some pretty devastating data highlighted that women were still firmly in their traditional place, the home, doing the bulk of care and domestic work.

In November 2020, Lyn Craig and Brendan Churchill of the University of Melbourne's School of Social and Political Sciences released the results of their survey of Australian parents in dual-earner couples, which they'd conducted in May during the first lockdown. They asked respondents how much time they spent in paid and unpaid labour, including both active and supervisory childcare, about their satisfaction with work-family balance and how their partner shared the load.

'Overall, paid work time was slightly lower and unpaid work time was very much higher during the lockdown than before,' Craig and Churchill concluded. But the breakdown by gender of who took on the 'much higher' load was not equal.

Women spent significantly more daily hours on housework and household management then men, 2.13 hours versus 1.66 hours.[75] What's more, during the lockdown women increased their *combined* time on household activities and active care by 2.8 hours, from 5.78 hours to 8.58 hours a day, while men increased theirs from 4.09 hours a day to 6.28 hours a day, leaving a gender gap of 36 per cent.[76]

Just think about that: if there's, say, fourteen to sixteen waking hours in the day, and if you're spending half or more on household work and care, that doesn't leave much time for paid work, let alone time to relax. No wonder women were so exhausted. No wonder so many felt they had no other choice – there's that loaded word for women again – but to ponder giving up paid work, to 'lean out'. You could put an actual number on women's epic distress and burnout: 8.58 hours a day.

The percentage of mothers who reported that they were 'extremely' dissatisfied with how they divided their time between paid work and unpaid work increased from just over 5 per cent to 24 per cent, and a third of mothers felt that they were doing 'much more' than their 'fair share' of housework and unpaid care during COVID-19.[77]

In short, women's dissatisfaction with how they divided their time between paid work and unpaid work increased *fivefold.* I repeat: women were *five times* as grumpy about the chore wars than they were before the pandemic. If this metric is not enough to spur structural change, then what is?

In December 2020, the Australian Bureau of Statistics released a survey into the household impacts of COVID-19, which showed remarkably similar results: while men did more childcare and unpaid domestic work during the pandemic than they did at the same time in the last year, women still did more.[78] Overall, women still did the lion's share of the heavy lifting at home.

The much hoped-for pandemic-fuelled gender revolution on the home front for women in heterosexual partnerships with children didn't materialise. Domestic democracy nirvana this was not. Bad news for anyone who had hoped the pandemic might prompt a fundamental change needed to gender inequities at home, and help reverse the trend of women leaving the workforce or going part time. And now what has so far been a slow decline is set to increase dramatically: I refer you to the Deloitte statistic in Chapter 3 again: one in four women is considering leaving the workforce … for good.[79]

In an increasingly politically polarised world, the importance of domestic democracy in underpinning gender equality at work is one issue that many people seem to agree on. The OECD has called the unequal distribution of unpaid labour '*the most* important gender equality issue of our time' (emphasis mine).[80] In a survey conducted by Women Deliver ahead of the 2021 Generation Equality Forum – a global gathering for gender equality convened by UN Women, and co-hosted that year by France and Mexico – the 'unequal distribution of unpaid care, domestic work, and parental responsibilities' was cited by respondents as the first or second biggest cause of gender inequality in thirteen of the seventeen countries surveyed.[81]

Yet despite this global recognition, we're stuck in the mud, both here in Australia and around the world. The pandemic experience has proven, yet again, just how 'sticky', to use the language of sociologists, gender norms at home are.

It is a well-known saying among the gender equality geeks of the world that without a revolution for men at home, there can be no revolution for women in the workplace. And yet, that revolution at home has not materialised. This point was well canvassed in journalist Annabel Crabb's now decade-old book, *The Wife Drought*, and later in her 2019 *Quarterly Essay*, 'Men at Work'. Crabb questions why the debate between work and family has always focused on the barriers that women face. She suggests that in our haste to resolve these barriers for women going into the workplace, we have forgotten that men face similarly obstructive barriers in getting out of the workplace.[82] And, I would add, it's a revolution that was always unlikely to be hastened by lean-in feminism's focus on boosting individual women's empowerment, rather than reforming the systems and structures that reinforce gendered norms at home.

So here we are. A 2019 report released by MenCare, a fatherhood campaign working towards childcare parity in forty-five nations, found that the unpaid care gap has decreased by just seven minutes (*just seven minutes*!) over the last fifteen years.[83] And a 2016 study that looked at time use surveys in nineteen countries found that the 'housework gap' largely stopped narrowing in the 1980s.[84]

Looking at a specific country examples, according to the US Time Use Survey, women who work outside the home shoulder 65 per cent of childcare responsibilities and their male partners 35 per cent – and those percentages have held steady for twenty years.[85]

In Australia, we don't know if the gap has changed over time because the Time Use Survey has not been conducted since 2006 when its funding was cut. And while the Australian

Time Use Survey has since been reinstated – thanks to a long feminist campaign – the results have not yet been published. That said, experts don't believe Australia will buck the international trend.

On the global level, at the current rate of change, it will be another seventy-five years before women as a group achieve domestic democracy, according to the MenCare report.[86] Women, who consistently do more unpaid care and domestic work than men – sometimes up to ten times as much – simply cannot wait that long.

This is an especially sad state of affairs, given this issue, the home front, was once upon a time on the feminist front line. That said, it is very possible that the galvanising effect of the pandemic – that fivefold increase in the extent to which women are decidedly grumpy about all this – could, once again, elevate this issue up the agenda of Australia's renewed, vibrant feminist campaigning.

* * *

In the 1970s, the domestic labour debate was at the forefront of feminist activism. It was then, just over a half a century ago in August 1970, that the Women's Strike for Equality in the US saw tens of thousands of women gather to protest in New York City to mark the fiftieth anniversary of women's suffrage in the United States. Officially sponsored by the National Organization for Women (NOW), the strike was the brainchild of Betty Friedan, who wanted an action that would show the American media the scope and power of second-wave feminism. Friedan's original idea for the 26 August protest was a national work stoppage in which women would cease cooking and cleaning in order to draw attention to the unequal distribution of domestic labour, an issue she had discussed at length in her 1963 classic, *The Feminine Mystique*. Participants held signs with slogans like 'Don't Iron While the Strike is Hot'.

The following year, 1971, Judy Syfers Brady wrote an iconic essay in the US feminist women's magazine *Ms.* entitled, 'I Want a Wife'. 'I want a wife who takes care of the children when they are sick, a wife who arranges to be around when the children need special care,' she wrote. 'I want a wife who will take care of my physical needs. I want a wife who will keep my house clean. A wife who will pick up after me.'[87]

'My God, who *wouldn't* want a wife?' was Brady's final lament, a plea that still resonates today. Decades later, Annabel Crabb would write in *The Wife Drought* that, 'working women are in an advanced, sustained, and chronically under-reported state of wife drought, and there is no sign of rain'.[88]

In 1972, an international collective of feminists from Italy, England and the US came together in Padua, Italy, to 'give voice to women's daily grind'. They founded the Wages for Housework movement, which highlighted the rank injustice of ignoring unpaid female domestic labour, without which modern economies could not function. Together they positioned housework as a capitalist abuse; it was capitalism that most profited from women's unpaid labour.

And then five years after the women's strike in the US, on the first day of the UN Decade for Women in 1975, the women of Iceland took the day off to demonstrate the importance of their work, waged and unwaged. Their slogan: 'When women stop, everything stops.'

How did we get from a situation where radical, direct action inspired a generation of women to take to the streets to protest domestic inequality and highlight the value and exploitation of women's unpaid labour, to a time – fifty years later – where we have seen decades of stasis on the home front and well-paid, privileged women, those who leaned in, were only too happy to exploit the cheap labour of mostly migrant and poor women to do the unpaid domestic work they couldn't or wouldn't do? This was lean-in feminism's tidy solution, and, fairly typically, it wasn't characterised by what I would call solidarity.

It's complicated.

Even before the pandemic, many theories tried to explain why the domestic burden between men and women with children in heterosexual relationships failed to shift in recent decades. The truth probably lies somewhere in a combination of those theories.

As Sally Howard wrote in her 2020 book *The Home Stretch: Why it's Time to Come Clean About Who Does the Dishes*, 'In the short generation from the 1970s to the 2010s, the emancipating feminist pronouncement "Girls can do anything!" was mangled into the edict "Women must do everything"'.[89] That was when feminism, as Barbara Ehrenreich wrote in her book *Nickel and Dimed* – after a few concessions – suffered a 'micro-defeat' in the home. And as a result, argued Ehrenreich, the 'problem' of gendered domestic labour was offloaded down a classed and racialised female labour line, and liberal feminism opened a new door for women: 'the servant's door'.[90]

Arlie Hochschild's foundational book, first published in 1989, *The Second Shift: Working Families and the Revolution at Home*, coined the phrase 'the second shift' to capture the fact that while women had made inroads into paid work, they hadn't ceded the burden of domestic work. Hochschild suggested that women's optimism was, partly, at fault. She wrote about female undergraduates in the 1980s who were optimistic that as men's attitudes changed, so too would men's behaviour. They were optimistic that they would find a man who planned to share the work at home.[91]

By 2015, it had become abundantly clear that change was anything but inevitable. Changes in attitudes did not necessarily translate into changes in behaviour. Journalist Claire Cain Miller captured this in an article for *The New York Times* in which she reported on a number of new studies indicating that 'millennial men aren't the dads they thought they would be'. Millennial men – then aged eighteen to early thirties – had much more egalitarian attitudes about family, career and gender roles inside marriage than generations before them, Miller explained, citing a variety of new research by social scientists. Yet they struggled to achieve their goals once they started families.

Miller reported that millennial men generally have more progressive beliefs about gender roles compared to men in other generations. Just 35 per cent of employed millennial men without children said they believed women should act as caregivers and men should be breadwinners in a family. But when these men have children, something changes: 53 per cent of millennial men with children said it was better for women and men to adopt traditional gender roles in their families.[92]

So millennial men, once they had children, changed their tune. But why?

There has been no shortage of the 'it's because men are a bit shit' (or variations on the theme) explanations. The Australian feminist Clementine Ford is a prominent champion of it (although she is by no means the only purveyor of this theory – in the States, Darcy Lockman, author of *All the Rage*, is another high-profile proponent). Ford even created the merch: she gives away 'Leave Your Husband' hats.

But the problem with this theory is that even if women leave all their unequal relationships or avoid marrying all the shit men, we will *still* have profound inequalities between men and women in every aspect of public and private life. The solution is not that simple. It requires us to look at both individual behaviour, and the systems and structures that influence that behaviour.

If some men are shit (and for the avoidance of doubt, some really are), we also have shit systems, workplace practices and public policy that preserve men's privilege, and, in many cases, particularly in Australia, work *against* men who want to go against the very gendered grain of work and home. A debate that presupposes the main or only cause of domestic inequality is men's uselessness and/or resistance to giving up privilege – basically their shittiness – fails to acknowledge some of the policy and workplace practices that *genuinely* make it difficult for men to counter the cultural norms about their role as a breadwinner. In short, exclusively blaming men for their choices is a bit like blaming women's choices for the gender pay gap. It does not take into account the broader context (including structural inequalities) that influences men's choices.

Consider this: a 2015 study published in the *American Sociological Review* journal – the first major examination of the effect workplace policies have on the choices of men and women – found that men and women aged eighteen to thirty-two have egalitarian attitudes about gender roles across all education and income levels, but when faced with a lack of family-friendly policies, most fall back on traditional roles. 'Women disproportionately benefit from the policies since they are expected to be caregivers, while men are stigmatised for using them,' the report found.[93]

What's more, according to the Australian Workplace Gender Equality Agency, just two in a hundred organisations have set targets for men's engagement in flexible work.[94] A 2016 study from the business consulting firm Bain and Co. found that men were twice as likely as women to have flexible work requests knocked back.[95] The Australian Human Rights Commission has found 27 per cent of fathers report experiencing discrimination related to parental leave and returning to work.[96]

'We have had a shift in attitudes, but there is a block, and you can see that in the empirical data showing that on the housework and caring front, not much is changing,' Leah Ruppanner, an associate professor of sociology at the University of Melbourne, who has written countless papers about domestic democracy, recently told me. 'The cultural or institutional aspect of this is so important, and if you have men who have a desire to do more but can't exercise that desire for fear of repercussions, we need to look at that.'

So, what's needed? We must learn the lessons of the pandemic and harness the increased rage at the current state of affairs on the home front into more effective, collective action that doesn't politely ask for, but collectively demands, radical change. As some have only half-jokingly suggested: maybe women should go on strike again. But this time around, it would be a powerful statement of progress if the dads of the world marched alongside them, because this is their fight too.

But what should they demand? Yes, more genuinely flexible workplace practices that benefit men and women and challenge the 'ideal worker' trope, usually a man with a wife at home who can subscribe to the culture of presenteeism that's rewarded with better pay and promotions. And yes, a genuine recognition of the value of care, and fair wages and conditions for those (mostly women) who do the paid care work as nannies, domestic cleaners, early years educators, aged care staff and disability support workers. Both are issues addressed elsewhere in this book.

But first and foremost, if we want that longed-for revolution at home we must reform Australia's now decade-old parental leave policy, which is one of the most unequal in the world in terms of the time offered to men and women. Until recently, Australia's paid parental leave still encouraged a single 'primary carer', who was eligible for eighteen weeks at minimum wage. The vast majority of that leave (99.5 per cent) was, therefore, taken by mothers who were deemed the primary carer. Fathers only got two weeks of dedicated partner leave, again paid at minimum wage.

In 2021, research from Marian Baird, Myra Hamilton and Andreea Constantin of the University of Sydney Business School finally said something that many of us had long been thinking: the scheme was a lemon. Okay, they put it slightly more diplomatically. 'Short secondary carer leave sets normative standards of fathers as "supporters" rather than recognising substantive involvement in care,' said Baird. 'Consequently, the scheme does not promote gender-egalitarian sharing of parental leave.'

As the research noted, 'While the introduction of the government scheme was a "giant leap", the 10 years since have seen modest "baby steps" towards greater gender equality in the availability and potential use of paid parental leave.'[97]

And while the Coalition government changed this situation in the March 2022 Budget, jettisoning the separate categories and consolidating all the leave into one lump families could choose to divide between mothers and fathers as they liked, experts warned that the change will only make the problem worse. It did nothing to give men an incentive to take more leave. Without something called a 'use it or lose it' provision that dedicates a portion of the leave to fathers that's lost if they don't take it, the pull of gendered norms and the fact that women tend to earn less than men mean that women would end up using all of the leave, and fewer fathers would take any leave at all. Brilliant.

There's the rub. Our current parental leave scheme, the major policy that influences the kinds of choices mums and dads in heterosexual relationships make, even in its slightly revised form, actually reinforces precisely the kinds of 'sticky' gender norms it could – and should – tackle. It simply needs to change, or nothing will at home. After decades of nibbling around the edges that has had zero impact, we know that now.

Here's just how impactful an improved parental leave scheme could be – one that includes a 'use it or lose it' provision for dads, and salary replacement rates for leave that make it economically viable to actually take it. Annabel Crabb's

*Quarterly Essay*, 'Men at Work: Australia's Parenthood Trap', chronicled how different countries and regions with the right parental leave policy transformed men's behaviour and increased men's uptake of parental leave in a very short period of time: Iceland from zero to 90 per cent in ten years; Norway from 2.4 to 70 per cent in four years; Germany from 5 to 34 per cent in seven years; and Quebec (the most comparable example for Australia, given its similar approach to social welfare) from 21.2 to 53.6 per cent in roughly thirteen years.[98] And evidence from around the world shows that fathers who take a significant period of parental leave when their baby is born are more likely to be more involved in caring and other housework years later.

Now that's a revolution worth striking for.

# 6.

# THROWING BABIES OUT WITH THE COVID BATHWATER

In early 2020, shortly after the dreaded virus arrived on our shores, Australians witnessed something rather extraordinary. federal education minister Dan Tehan announced that all childcare would be free for the next three months, with the possibility that the new arrangements could remain in place for as long as six months.

Childcare, or as geeks like me prefer to call it, 'early years education and care', has long been a topical issue for parents in Australia. The nation has consistently ranked as having some of the most expensive childcare in the world; only Switzerland is more expensive.[99] Fees have increased by 14.7 per cent since the last election in 2019. There have been increasingly urgent calls for reform for years.

For the person earning the lowest wage in a two-parent household, generally the mother, the invisible cost can be even higher. The expense of childcare imposes an effective tax as high as 70 per cent on the second-earner's salary if they work more than three days a week.[100] As a result, employed women in Australia are more likely to work part time than employed women in any other member of the thirty-eight-nation OECD, apart from Japan, Switzerland and the Netherlands. When asked why they are unable to work more hours, almost half of the women surveyed in 2018–19 by the Australian Bureau of Statistics nominated 'caring for children'.[101]

It's worth noting that women didn't cite a 'lack of confidence' or any of the other 'problems' that lean-in feminism has long aimed to solve. This was a significant, practical issue that needed a high-level, structural response. One that had not been forthcoming from a nearly decade-old Coalition government that did nothing but tinker around the edges of childcare by increasing subsidies, only to see those subsidies, predictably, eaten up when the childcare providers raised fees.

The profits lined the pockets of the many commercial, private providers of early education, while doing nothing to address the issue for mothers on the ground.[102]

But then the pandemic, yet again, disrupted the status quo.

Just weeks into the first wave of the pandemic and the first lockdown, childcare was 'on the ropes', as the long-time early years education campaigner Lisa Bryant put it, and more to the point, 'nurses and doctors can't work without it'.[103] The pandemic focused our collective minds, and – at long last – the minds of reluctant Liberal ministers.

By then, any parent who could had pulled their child out of childcare. And the ones who hadn't were the ones who needed their children to attend so they could continue to do their jobs. But with only a few children bringing in the fees and subsidies that keep early years education and care services afloat, many services couldn't afford to keep operating.

The services had high wage bills and high rents but low occupancy rates; many were on the brink of closing.

When and if Australians ever emerged from lockdown – and at that stage we didn't know how long it might last – there was a real possibility that there would be far fewer childcare centres for parents to send their children to. How big was the risk? A subsequent review found that 30 per cent of providers faced closure and another 25 per cent were not sure they would ever recover, even once the virus crisis passed.[104]

If this was allowed to happen, the knock-on impact on women's workforce participation rates would be devastating. With Australia's deeply entrenched gender norms regarding the division of unpaid care and household labour in the home, it would inevitably be women who were called back to hearth and home.

'These are extraordinary times,' the minister told the ABC's Patricia Karvelas shortly after he announced the measures.[105]

As I watched at home, I was surprised. This was the same Dan Tehan who – less than a year earlier – had called Labor's pre-election childcare proposals 'a fast track to a socialist, if not a communist, economy'. Those proposals included subsidies that would have seen free childcare offered to lower-income families and a commitment to address the appallingly low wages of early years educators in this female-dominated sector.

At the time Tehan made those comments likening universal childcare to communism, I took the opportunity, writing in *The Sydney Morning Herald*, to remind the education minister that we could, in fact, learn a thing or two from the communists in relation to childcare. After reunification in Germany, I wrote, the former West Germany learned lessons from the former East Germany's universal childcare system.

Those lessons helped avert an impending demographic crisis: birth rates in West Germany were falling because women felt they could not both have a child and continue to work if childcare wasn't readily available and affordable. (This is an issue, incidentally, that Australia is also facing.)

Later, in 2013, Germany declared that every child over the age of one had a legal right to a space in a public childcare facility. Five years later, Germany's highest court took that mandate one step further and ruled parents could sue for lost wages if they could not find a place in a public childcare facility. Now that's what I call extraordinary.[106]

By early 2020, it was a whole new world in Australia for Dan Tehan and the Coalition government that had hitherto fiercely resisted change.

There's nothing like a global health crisis to shift deeply entrenched, and downright stubbornly held ideological views about essential services, particularly the kind of essential services and 'care infrastructure' that underpin women's ability to do paid work.

This wasn't the first time a global crisis had upended how we think about childcare and whether mothers should be tethered to the home to provide that care for free.

* * *

In the United States during World War II – another time of great disruption – women were needed in manufacturing jobs as men were shipped off to the front, so the Roosevelt administration funded a network of childcare centres. Without those centres, Rosie the Riveter would have never have donned her kerchief and taken up tools on the wartime production line.[107]

That childcare cost just US$10 a day in today's dollars. The quality was high, it attracted and retained trained teachers, and it had low child-to-teacher ratios. Research showed it improved children's education,[108] employment[109] and earnings later in life, in addition to the obvious immediate imperative to increase and support women's workforce participation rates and boost overall economic productivity.

These are all outcomes that Australia, coronavirus or no coronavirus, might consider worthy goals in and of themselves.

Unfortunately, US president Harry S. Truman shut the childcare centres down shortly after Japan surrendered. And in doing so, the US missed a valuable opportunity to capitalise on a well-resourced, world-class childcare system that could have further underpinned the country's post-war economic recovery. Only more recently, as out-of-control costs and a lack of availability turned America's 'childcare crisis into an economic crisis'[110] of lower workforce participation and productivity, did the issue once again attain national prominence. Ahead of the 2020 US presidential elections, most Democratic presidential hopefuls pitched the return of universal childcare to voters. Another crisis. Another shift.

In Australia, the valuable opportunity was also, initially, missed. By June 2020, the early years sector had 'snapped back' (the term Tehan preferred for what should happen), with the free childcare coming to an end and the system returning to the complicated and inadequate subsidy scheme that had been in place prior to COVID.

Childcare, apart from being expensive, is also difficult to access, especially in remote and regional areas.[111] A 2022 study from Victoria University found that about nine million Australians, or about a third of the population, live in a neighbourhood classified as a 'childcare desert'.[112]

When I first moved to Australia in 2013, I thought I would never work again. I could only find care for my children in neighbourhoods far from my house, which resulted in a one-and-a-half-hour round trip just to drop them off at care. How would I find a job that allowed me – or my husband – to rock up to work at 10.30 am and leave at 4.30 pm? I joined Australia's army of part-time mums who had no other choice but to stay home with their kids, due to the high cost and inaccessibility of childcare.

What's more, 2020 was not the first time the Coalition government had resisted meaningful reform in the face of overwhelming evidence of the need to act: the government's 2018 childcare package of reforms was partly designed to help families work more, but the benefits were 'too modest to matter', according to Rob Bray, Ben Phillips, Ilan Katz and Matthew Gray.[113] When the package was initially announced in 2017, then prime minister Malcolm Turnbull described it as 'the most significant reform to the early education and care system in 40 years'.[114] Not so much.

Bray and Phillips' team, which was commissioned by the government to evaluate the package, found that while for a majority of families the package had a positive financial benefit, this tended to be relatively modest. And the policy had little impact on longer term costs, access, flexibility or workforce engagement.

Later, in the 2022 Women's Budget Statement, the Morrison government yet again tried to make a virtue of its tinkering around the edges. Just days after the release of the research highlighting the prevalence of childcare 'deserts', the government's sole additional childcare measure was to announce funding for twenty new childcare centres in under-served areas in the 2022 Budget. Twenty! They seemed determined to continue to piss in the wind of a hurricane.

The extent to which a fundamental shift in Australia's approach to early years education could – and should – underpin the post-COVID economic recovery faded into the Coalition government's rear-view mirror as the more immediate crisis of lockdowns passed. But not everyone was prepared to let it go.

* * *

The first sign that change was in the air was the launch of the Thrive by Five campaign in September 2020, with the goal of making Australia's early learning childcare system high quality and universally accessible. Backed by the Minderoo Foundation, the campaign is led by the philanthropist Nicola Forrest, who is married to the mining magnate Andrew Forrest.

That there was a new organisation dedicated to campaigning for universal, accessible childcare didn't surprise me. What floored me was watching a well-funded campaigning organisation launch into the space with such a broad and unprecedented alliance of supporters from across the political spectrum. The whole thing had an 'it's time' quality to it right from the start.

The group included traditional advocates of childcare such as Georgie Dent, executive director of The Parenthood advocacy group, and Michele O'Neil, president of the ACTU, alongside former Liberal politicians Kate Carnell and

Julie Bishop. Bishop pointed out that early years education is a 'powerful driver of good social and economic outcomes', and that 'it should be seen as an investment rather than a cost'. Carnell talked about how in her previous role as the Australian small business and family enterprise ombudsman she had seen too many women unable to dedicate the time to grow their businesses because of the cost of childcare. Both Liberal women broke ranks with their tribe to state the obvious.

A year later, in November 2021, Forrest would take her advocacy one step further, convening a powerful group of senior businesswomen, former politicians and community leaders – another broad alliance of somewhat unlikely bedfellows – in the newly formed Women for Progress coalition to demand sweeping improvements to address women's lagging economic security and put women at the centre of Australia's 'build back better' economic recovery. The twenty-three prominent women included Julie Bishop, ex-Labor MPs Kate Ellis and Jenny Macklin, former Sydney lord mayor Lucy Turnbull, Aboriginal and Torres Strait Islander social justice commissioner June Oscar, Diversity Council of Australia chair Ming Long, businesswomen Wendy McCarthy and Carol Schwartz, and Michele O'Neil.

As well as calling for big government investment in universal quality childcare, the group also lobbied for increased paid parental leave of up to one year, paid family violence leave and legislative change to mandate public reporting of the gender pay gap. 'We have to make workforce participation easier for women, not harder ... it comes down to supporting families so that women can re-enter the workforce, because we are losing our educated women and it is affecting our GDP. This is a national prosperity problem,' said Forrest.[115]

There was a sense of momentum and urgency to discussions around early years education and care that had been completely absent before. And for good reason: despite a 'record spend' of $10.3 billion in the 2021–22 financial year (as the Morrison government was so keen to regularly remind Australian parents), Australia's childcare system was in crisis and fundamentally dysfunctional following the pandemic.

The COVID-19 crisis had shown the fragility of our early learning and care system. The federal government had to implement two rescue packages for the sector in two years, and a further rescue package was considered to deal with the Omicron variant surge. The pandemic also showed that early childhood education and care is an essential service and must be reformed to meet families' needs in a post-COVID Australia.

Investment in early childhood development is critical for Australia's economic and social recovery from the COVID crisis. It is critical for workforce participation and future productivity. It will accelerate our recovery; create a healthier, happier and more productive nation; and make our society more resilient to future shocks. This all adds up to what many economists call a 'double dividend' of investment, bringing both social and economic benefits for every dollar invested into early years education and care.

The question now is, will the new Labor government meet the moment? Or will they go the way of Truman and 'waste a crisis'?

# 7.

# FAIR GAME: SAFETY AT WORK

There is a concept in psychology of a 'flashbulb memory', a highly vivid and detailed snapshot of a moment in time when a consequential, surprising and emotionally stirring piece of news is heard for the very first time. We will all likely have a few such moments over the course of our lives.

As a native New Yorker, I obviously count the events of 9/11 as such a memory that I will never forget. I can recount the events of that day in vivid detail. More recently, I can also remember exactly where I was and how I felt the day the Harvey Weinstein story first broke in *The New York Times* – exposing his decades of abuse of power and predation of women.

I can also remember the overwhelming feeling I had – even before the floodgates of #MeToo opened – that this would give rise to something big, something that would fundamentally shift the way we think about women's safety at work and what we believed was within our power to change.

When the story first broke on 5 October 2017, I was at the annual *Women's Agenda* Leadership Awards in Sydney where Professor Gillian Triggs, Australia's former human rights commissioner, was being inducted into the Women's Agenda Hall of Fame. Triggs had recently stepped down from her role, admitting that taking on the government had not been particularly good for her career, and she was feeling feisty.

The feeling in the room was electric. The news coming out of the US was so staggering you could almost feel the righteous anger, an emotion that would be later channelled into the years of advocacy and work towards change that would follow. And you could also sense that there was a collective understanding that we would have to upend much of the 'business as usual' orthodoxy in regards to women's safety and equality at work that had, for too long, narrowly defined the scope of our advocacy and solutions.

This was *the* moment, the first since I had arrived in Australia more than a decade before, when I felt the ends of the threads of the lean-in feminist orthodoxy in Australia beginning to fray.

Looking back, I can't help but think that it was no coincidence Professor Triggs' acceptance speech on that day touched upon the need to challenge that orthodoxy. She talked about her experience coming of age in the 1960s and her former belief that if you gave women an education, you would unlock many doors for them. She noted that while Australian women topped the international league tables for educational attainment, Australia had slipped from fifteenth to forty-sixth in the World Economic Forum Global Gender Gap Report in just a decade. (Australia has since slipped even further, now sitting in fiftieth place.)

Then Triggs drew on her own experience of 'playing the game', getting her hair done and wearing some unfortunate oversized shoulder pads in the 1980s, and subscribing to a corporate feminist playbook – well before Sandberg's manifesto to that end was published. But now that she was no longer employed by the government, she wanted to ask this question of herself and others: 'Are we too measured? Too databased? Too calm under fire? Perhaps it's time to be a bit more vulgar? Let's stand up for what we believe in!'

In that moment, I sensed – for myself and others – a decided frustration with what 'playing the game' in regard to gender equality and women's safety had achieved. What had playing by the rules delivered?

Women had heeded the call to arm themselves with education to succeed in the workplace. Australian women were now among the most highly educated in the world – as Triggs mentioned in her speech – but when they entered the workforce in large numbers in the 1980s and 90s, that investment they had made in the promise of a better future was squandered. It did not translate into the success – albeit 'success' defined in very narrow terms – that was promised.

Women in Australia were still under-represented in the highest ranks of business and politics, and they had some of the highest part-time work rates in the OECD. All too often, they were driven off course onto the 'mummy track' of poor pay and poor prospects as the so-called motherhood penalty bit. The high cost of childcare and the dominant cultural expectation that women should carry the load of unpaid and low-paid care work underpinned this trend.

Women believed the mantra 'what gets measured gets managed', which launched a thousand feminist data ships chronicling everything from the gender pay gap and rates of violence against women, to women's lack of representation in powerful roles and the chores gap. If we measured the size of any particular women's issue, action to address it would surely follow.

Few asked this question: what about the things we don't measure? Does that mean they're not worth managing? For example, the size of the gender pay gap for culturally and linguistically diverse and Black women. Or the fact that there is no data or information on the superannuation situation of women with disability.[116]

Later, that message was complemented by another: rather than shout louder about structural injustice, women should further invest in themselves, bolster their confidence, silence their supposed inner critic of self-doubt. Women played by those rules too – they 'leaned in'.

But were women in the workplace any safer?

We wouldn't have to wait long for the answer to that question. The results of the next Australian Human Rights Commission survey looking at the rates of sexual harassment were released a year after the Weinstein story broke, in 2018. The answer was sobering: rates of sexual harassment in Australia had *increased* from one in four people when the survey was last conducted in 2012 to one in three people in 2018, and rates of sexual harassment were consistently higher among women than men and even higher among Indigenous women, women of colour and disabled women.[117] We had measured, but we had clearly not managed. That increase, curiously, mapped almost directly on to the period of federal Coalition leadership.

What's more, half of the victims had experienced similar harassment before, and a substantial proportion experienced negative consequences as a result, such as impacts on mental health or stress, victimisation or the loss of their job. And this situation was certainly not the result of the rogue 'confused', handsy bloke at a Christmas party, as some would have us believe, but part of a widespread, troubling pattern of behaviour. Disturbingly, the survey revealed that the reporting of workplace sexual harassment continued to be low, with only 17 per cent of people who experienced sexual harassment at work in the previous five years making a formal report or complaint about the harassment.[118]

Anyone looking to individual women alone to manage this particular crisis by speaking out and taking a claim to the employment tribunal, by holding their perpetrators and the workplaces that protected them to account, would be waiting for a very long time. We needed another way forward.

Another survey published the same year, a nationally representative survey of young Australian working women's attitudes to work and the future of work, was even more sobering.[119] When asked what 'matters most' in a job, respect in the workplace ranked first (80 per cent), even higher than decent pay (65 per cent). A full two-thirds of respondents said there wasn't gender equality in the workplace and around half (53 per cent) were not optimistic that gender equality in the workplace would improve in the next ten years.

For young women to list respect in the workplace among the things they valued most, and to say it mattered more than decent pay, was just heartbreaking – it's such a basic right. That we had failed to achieve this right for the next generation of women, and that so few were optimistic that things would change, highlighted the failure of those gender equality advocates who had pursued individually focused, lean-in feminist solutions for nearly a decade

What had a 'databased', 'measured' approach actually delivered? A perpetuation of the status quo and a younger generation of women entering the workplace for whom the attainment of the basic principle of respect was more important than decent pay.

Reflecting on this, I was reminded of an anecdote which I think captures a bit of what Gillian Triggs was alluding to that day. The legendary American feminists Flo Kennedy and Gloria Steinem used to travel the US together as speaking partners in the 1970s. One day Kennedy, famous for what some dubbed 'verbal karate', pulled Steinem aside and ticked her off for being too reliant on facts and figures to make her case. Steinem, it would seem, was one of the early believers of the 'what gets measured gets managed' mantra. Kennedy told Steinem, 'Honey, when you are lying in a ditch with a truck on your ankle, you do not send someone to the library to find out how much the truck weighs. You get it off!'

A change of approach was needed.

That change would come as the #MeToo wave broke belatedly over Australia in 2021. But in fact we can trace the origins to 2017, when a world-first sexual harassment inquiry, led by sex discrimination commissioner Kate Jenkins, was commissioned by the Turnbull government. That inquiry, which came to be known as *Respect@Work*, was released in early 2020, and it was forensic in nature and galvanising.

It was informed by an epic sixty consultations and drew on 460 submissions from legal services, unions, women's services, academic experts and, most importantly, victims. And it was underpinned by the fourth national survey on sexual harassment in Australian workplaces, which, as I've already canvassed, worryingly found that rates of sexual harassment had *increased*. Yes, we had sent our metaphorical feminist librarian in the form of Kate Jenkins off to the library to measure the size of the problem. But she also came back with the blueprint for the crane that could lift the truck off us.

Described as 'revolutionary', the report's fifty-five recommendations covered everything from a more robust legal and regulatory framework to a more holistic support system for those who had experienced sexual harassment. Most importantly, the report's central recommendation called for a 'positive duty' on employers to prevent sexual harassment from happening in the first place.[120]

Billed as a game changer, the positive duty would take the burden off victims.

As the last few years have demonstrated, women who have spoken out publicly, or had their stories co-opted by an insensitive media, have paid a high price for coming forward. How high was that price? A 2021 study published by Time's Up and the Institute for Women's Policy Research sought to nail down exactly how much it cost victims.[121] Victims said they faced expenses anywhere from tens of thousands to hundreds of thousands of dollars. For one woman working in the well-paid, male-dominated construction industry, the lifetime cost could reach US$1.3 million. Even someone forced out of a low-wage job in the fast-food industry saw a financial fallout totalling $125,600.

Now, employers would be responsible for taking *proactive* steps to *prevent* sexual harassment and assault from happening in the first place. Responsibility for tackling sexual harassment would no longer rest solely on individual women's shoulders, whose only option was to combat it via expensive and emotionally gruelling individual legal action. Employers would have a legal duty to prevent it from happening, and Australia's sex discrimination commissioner would be given the powers (and resources) to enforce that duty.

The sense of urgency and the mandate for broad structural change – not just another measurement exercise that disappeared under the surface of the waves of #MeToo – were clear. This was a breakthrough moment, shifting the burden from individual women to those with the power to shape systems and structures, the very systems and structures that had conspired to protect powerful perpetrators. Leaning in wasn't going to solve this problem, certainly not a problem so deeply embedded in systems of power.

But, sadly, the *Respect@Work* inquiry's recommendations were so revolutionary that they landed in (and stayed buried in) then attorney-general Christian Porter's drawer for more than a year. Then, in 2021, a series of events reinvigorated calls for that kind of radical change against an even more incendiary backdrop.

In January 2021, child sexual abuse survivor Grace Tame was named Australian of the Year, and a month later former political staffer Brittany Higgins bravely came forward to tell her story of an alleged sexual assault in Parliament House. In March, Christian Porter identified himself as the minister at the centre of a historic rape allegation, an allegation he vigorously denied, and by July of that year two former MPs from either side of the aisle, ex-Labor minister Kate Ellis and ex-Liberal MP Julia Banks, had penned books exposing the dark underbelly of sexism in our nation's parliament.

These events and the March4Justice protests across the country they inspired led to renewed calls for the Morrison government to respond to all of Jenkins' *Respect@Work* inquiry recommendations, including the positive duty. There were calls, too, for the government to commission another specific inquiry into Parliament House as a workplace.

By the time the Coalition government finally took action in September 2021 on *Respect@Work*, in the form of the Sex Discrimination and Fair Work (Respect at Work) Amendment Bill, it legislated to implement just six of the fifty-five recommendations.

'It's devastating to see a real opportunity for positive change be denied for all the working women in this country,' Brittany Higgins said after the passage of the Bill. Catherine Marriott, who filed a complaint with the National Party about deputy prime minister Barnaby Joyce's behaviour, allegations he denied, concurred. 'I have no words for how frustrated, hopeless, sad.... words escape me... I am at this!' she tweeted. 'This was a real opportunity to say sexual assault and harassment in the workplace is not ok. [sic]'[122]

But Jenkins would not be deterred. 'I'm not letting it go,' a determined Jenkins told me late last year in reference to her game-changing *Respect@Work* recommendations that were yet to be adopted, including the positive duty. 'There has been a shift,' she said. 'Now I want to see courageous leadership to match the courage of the women who have spoken out.'

While the Morrison government resisted implementing all of the recommendations in *Respect@Work*, it did bow to pressure and commission an inquiry into Parliament House as a workplace, also to be led by Jenkins. The results of that inquiry, published as *Set the Standard*, were jaw-dropping.[123]

'I was sexually harassed multiple times, sexually assaulted, bullied and terrorised,' one parliamentary staffer told the inquiry. 'And I was told that if I ever sought help or spoke about what happened to me my professional reputation and personal life would be destroyed.'

Another anonymous contributor described working in Parliament House as going on a school camp in year nine with naughty schoolboys who 'think everyone's fair game'.

Yet another said, 'It is a man's world, and you are reminded of it every day, thanks to the looks up and down you get, to the representation in the parliamentary chambers, to the preferential treatment politicians give senior male journalists.'

And a fourth recounted this horrific experience: '[T]he MP sitting beside me leaned over. Also thinking he wanted to tell me something, I leaned in. He grabbed me and stuck his tongue down my throat. The others all laughed. It was revolting and humiliating.'

Altogether, the 1723 individual women and men and thirty-three organisations who contributed to the inquiry painted a damning picture of the workplace culture at the very apex of power in Australia: one in three parliamentary staffers said they had been sexually harassed; just over half of all people currently working in Commonwealth parliamentary workplaces had experienced at least one incident of bullying, sexual harassment, or actual or attempted sexual assault; and rates of harassment and bullying were, not surprisingly, higher among women.

Even more shameful: at the press conference in late 2021 to launch the inquiry's final report, Jenkins told the assembled media that this kind of sexual harassment and assault in our nation's parliament was so pervasive that 'women told us they felt "lucky" if they had not *directly* experienced sexual harassment and assault'. As one contributor quoted in the very first line of the report stated: 'This is Parliament. It should set the standard for workplace culture, not the floor of what culture should be.'

Indeed.

Again, Jenkins' inquiry went well beyond simply measuring the problem. She proposed twenty-eight recommendations for radical change, including a code of conduct to be enforced by an Independent Parliamentary Standards Commission and a push for gender parity to change the workplace culture within federal parliament. And she was determined to see the implementation of *all* of those recommendations, taking steps to pre-empt any Morrison government attempt to cherry-pick her recommendations (as happened to the *Respect@Work* inquiry), stating clearly that the twenty-eight recommendations were 'a package, mutually reinforcing and complementary and therefore should not be cherry picked for implementation'.

'My sense was that this had been building,' Jenkins told me of the events that preceded Australia's #MeToo reckoning and informed her two inquiries. 'What's happened in the last few years was the result of a build-up over many, many years.' According to Jenkins, the 1990s and 2000s saw progress stall on gender equality and women's safety at work. Women, she said, were essentially told, 'You've got the laws (in reference to the 1984 *Sex Discrimination Act*), now stop whining ... it's up to you to go and succeed.' Hmmm, where have I heard that before?

Now in 2022, Australia is finally on the brink of real change. That's after years of sexual harassment and assault at work dominating the headlines as never before, with story after harrowing story of abuse – those of Tessa Sullivan, Eryn Jean Norvill, Chelsey Potter, Dhanya Mani, Ashleigh Raper, Julia Szlakowski and Brittany Higgins, to name a few.

And the pandemic has only heightened the expectation that we will tackle everything that undermines women's economic security by forcing them to 'lean out' of work, which sexual harassment so clearly does. Roughly half of women who have experienced sexual harassment say that the harassment caused them to leave jobs or switch careers.[124]

'We've created the space for people to share their stories,' Dr Sonia Palmieri, an Australian National University gender and politics expert, told me about the events of the last few years. 'After so long sweeping it under the carpet, that's a fundamental shift.'

In 2022, we have the tools to remove this particular truck, not just the statistics to measure its size. This movement, this wave of activism, has yielded more than measurement, and it's a blueprint for what full-throated collective activism can deliver on many fronts for women at work; it has yielded very specific solutions drawn from the hard graft of consultation, consensus building and the incredible bravery of the many who spoke out. Women are demanding change as a powerful, collective force. They are saying 'enough'. That's different. While it's not new, it's been sorely lacking on this scale for far too long.

# CONCLUSION
# A NEW DEAL FOR WOMEN AT WORK

In May 2022, the people of Australia, and particularly the women of Australia, delivered a verdict on the Coalition government's almost ten years in power. In an unprecedented result, they elected a sizeable crossbench, including the so-called Teals, moderate women candidates who campaigned on climate change, gender equality and empathetic leadership, and more Greens. Both would change the electoral face of the nation. The result was a verdict on many aspects of the Coalition government, from its abysmal record on climate change to its reignition of the culture wars and its utter disregard for gender equality.

At the ballot box, women abandoned the Coalition in droves, clearly rejecting the 'choice' feminist solutions it had on offer, the kinds of solutions that largely blamed women for their own inequality and left it to them to fix the problem, on an individual basis.

This was a government for whom gender inequality was all about women's 'choices' (in the same way that unemployment was all about the unemployed person's 'choices', or that those who couldn't afford to buy a home should just 'get a good job', as then Treasurer Joe Hockey said in 2015). And those 'choices' were not in any way influenced by the context in which they were made.

The women of Australia, however, didn't buy it. This was despite the Coalition government's $348.5 million Women's Budget Statement investing in various #GirlBoss initiatives designed to help women into leadership positions in 'better paid' male-dominated industries and entrepreneurship.[125] It offered nothing to tackle the undervaluing of women's work in female-dominated caring professions, while there was an insultingly tiny initiative to tackle the ongoing childcare crisis, and the proposed parental leave initiative was projected to do more harm than good. Many women also strongly suspected that the relatively small reduction in the gender pay gap during the Coalition's time in office had nothing to do with Coalition government policies aimed at increasing (some) women's wages; the gap narrowed because men's wages decreased.

Women would simply not be gaslit into believing they were more economically secure when the reality of their daily lives told them something different, especially for the women on the front line of the pandemic in undervalued caring professions. Nor would women be persuaded they were better off when many were all too aware of the fact that women over the age of fifty-five were the fastest growing portion of the homeless population.

Women raged, they marched, and then they voted.

In the early days after the election, various prominent media commentators attempted to interpret the meaning of this result. Where had the Coalition gone wrong with women? Unfortunately, much of that early analysis focused on where the Coalition government had gone wrong with professional women, not women who – in all their diversity – delivered this scathing verdict. Some, including me, read this to mean privileged, largely white corporate women, as if that was the only cohort of female voters that mattered.

My response, then and now, is that such an analysis credits a strain of lean-in feminism in Australia for the election result when that same strain of feminism was, in my view, complicit in a lost decade of inaction. What's more, it bypasses women's anger, what they were demanding and why. It also prevents us from learning the lessons of an election held in the midst of a pandemic that disproportionately impacted women. If the women of Australia saw fit to turf out the Coalition government and its lean-in feminist mantras, it is incumbent upon the rest of us who claim to advocate on behalf of women in Australia to learn those lessons too.

The 2022 election result revealed a deeper shift, one that has significant implications if we are serious about learning the lessons of the pandemic and crafting a new deal for women at work, *all* women in *all* forms of paid and unpaid work. A new, powerful, collective political force has been unleashed that could drive change, and it's one that's been a long time coming.

When I first moved to Australia nearly a decade ago, I was puzzled that political parties of all persuasions weren't more concerned about the so-called 'women's vote'. In my more recent experience in the UK, the major political parties' desire to court this vital, decisive vote was rather useful to anyone advocating on behalf of women.

In 2006, while I was working at the UK's Equal Opportunity Commission (EOC), we published a report, *Sex Equality and the Modern Family: The New Political Battleground*. That report showed just how important women voters were. It estimated that if only women had voted at the previous general election, in 2005, the Labour government's majority would have been over ninety seats, and if only men had voted, it would have been reduced to a narrow twenty-three.

The report essentially highlighted the importance of the 'gender gap' in voting habits, which had widened over time as women as a group had become more highly educated and entered the workforce in larger numbers. They tended to – as a group – vote for political parties with policies that spoke to their specific interests and rights. The EOC report went on to explain that 'a new political battleground was opening up' and that all political parties faced a 'credibility gap' on policies that affect parents and carers, but that gap was largest for the Conservatives.

David Cameron had just been elected the Conservative opposition leader the year before, and in addition to burnishing the Conservative Party's credentials on the environment he was also keen to persuade women that his party cared about women's representation, the gender pay gap and the disproportionate burden of caring responsibilities that usually fell on women's shoulders.

One headline from a London *Times* article about the EOC report read, 'Cameron Knows that Women Make His Party Swing'. In fact, it was a Conservative government, under David Cameron's leadership, that announced an intention to mandate equal pay reporting, which was subsequently introduced by Theresa May in 2017. This is something we still don't have in Australia.

The women's vote was not yet decisive at this time in Australia – and the Coalition government believed it could, therefore, remain indifferent or downright hostile to women.

My puzzlement at this state of affairs in Australia prompted me to do a bit of digging into the history of the gender gap in Australian politics, and what I discovered was rather surprising. Until 2001, Australian women bucked the international trend that saw women with increased education and workforce participation rates move towards Labour or Social Democratic parties. Here, women remained loyal to the Liberal Party longer – and helped keep them in power.

But then that started to change. The Liberal Party realised it had a 'woman problem' somewhat belatedly in 2015. Alarm bells started to go off, and that year the Menzies Research Centre, a conservative think tank, published its first report, *Gender and Politics*.[126] One of the report's authors, Nick Cater, said there were 'some indications' female voters wanted to see women representing them in parliament, and would vote accordingly. 'Right up until the turn of the century … [the Liberals] had a clear lead when it came to women voters,' Cater said. 'Now it's neck and neck, since the 2001 election it's pretty much even. We don't have any hard evidence on this, but we do have a correlation.'[127]

Suffice to say, after the 2022 election, we now have some 'hard evidence'.

Some thought this particular chicken would come home to roost at the 2019 election, and that the 'women's vote' would finally tip the outcome of a federal election in Australia and prove decisive. But it didn't happen. At the time, Professor Ian McAllister of the ANU attributed this to what he saw as Australia's utilitarian political culture, as opposed to a rights-based culture. 'People tend to view the state as something to deliver goods and services, benefits, regulation,' he told me, 'whereas people in Britain and the US see the state as something that delivers personal freedom and human rights … so it's largely a question of political culture.'[128]

Fast forward to the year 2022, when Jenna Price interviewed McAllister for *The Sydney Morning Herald* a few months before the election, and his opinion had shifted dramatically.[129] The women's vote was shifting for a few reasons, McAllister told Price. Among them: women understand the pressures of the workforce because they are in it. And after two years of the pandemic, they were 'truly, madly, deeply in it'. McAllister predicted that in the upcoming election, anything related to women would resonate: 'It's going to be big … women in the workplace, political representation of women in Parliament, social issues.'

Yes, indeed. It was big.

Women in all their diversity traded their 'utilitarian' political jumpsuits for 'I am a woman and I vote' T-shirts. And in doing so, they ushered in a new era of a 'rights-based' political culture that any political party now ignores at its peril.

After more than two years of the pandemic, everything that women have experienced on the work front, on the home front, and in regard to their safety both at work and home, has helped expedite this shift. And it's huge. Importantly, the pandemic also hastened women's disillusionment with lean-in feminism and their belief that it had the answers.

Together, these two phenomena have helped drive change, and, I believe, will continue to drive change into the future. There's a powerful, collective political force demanding action to address the undervaluing of women's work and the crisis of care it has ushered in; action to tackle the exorbitant cost of childcare and the vital role it plays in enabling women to work outside the home; action to help level the domestic playing field through public policy that actually drives change at home; meaningful reform to prevent sexual harassment from happening in the first place and a much-improved response that supports victims when it does happen; action to address the myriad injustices (including intersecting forms of gender, race, disability and gender identity discrimination) that drive the gender pay gap that results in too many women living in poverty or being homeless; and action on all these fronts and more to, quite literally, save women's sanity.

# ACKNOWLEDGEMENTS

Throughout the past decade, when the broader political landscape and mainstream feminist discourse in Australia hampered efforts to promote gender equality and deliver the basic human right of safety, many activists, service providers, policy experts, academics and others have continued to work at the coalface, sometimes pushed to the margins. They endured threats to their funding, bullying at the hands of the Australian Charities and Not-for-profits Commission, lest they engage in full-throated advocacy, and more.

I want to acknowledge their work and perseverance. You are too many to name individually. In the course of my career in Australia working in the non-profit women's sector and the media, I have had the great privilege of meeting many of you in person and collaborating with a few of you on some worthy projects. It is *your* work in these less-than-ideal circumstances that has built a bridge to this moment, and change is always born from the collective efforts of many, not any single individual. I know you know that. You know who you are. I see you. Thank you.

As for my journey to this book, I would like to thank my husband Richard and my girls, Esme and Isla. Richard once joked that I was in danger of becoming 'emotionally unemployed' in reference to his great capacity to carry more than his fair share of the emotional labour and mental load required to keep our family's show on the road. He is a role model for other men and fathers, though he gets terribly cross when I point this out publicly and will, no doubt, be annoyed by this acknowledgement. My girls remind me each and every day why we're trying to build a better future for women and girls.

My parents Karl-Heinz Ziwica and Jutta Ziwica made it possible for me to pursue my dream to become a journalist, and to later to marry my passion for gender equality with a career in the media through my formative internship at *Ms.* magazine, which lit a fire that's still burning twenty-five years later.

Thank you Sarah Wootton and Lisa Wheildon for taking a chance on an unconventional job candidate and giving me those first jobs in London and Melbourne, both were foundational to my understanding of gender equality and the drivers of violence against women. Thank you both for continuing to mentor me long after you were no longer my bosses, when you instead became valued friends.

Finally, thank you to my many former colleagues and 'stakeholders' at the UK Human Rights Commission and Our Watch who taught me so much. To Sheila Wild in particular, you taught me everything I know about the gender pay gap. I learnt at the feet of the master.

# NOTES

1 Sheryl Sandberg, *Lean In: Women, Work, and the Will to Lead*, New York: Knopf, 2013.

2 Meraiah Foley and Rae Cooper, 'Workplace gender equality in the post-pandemic era: Where to next?', *Journal of Industrial Relations*, Vol. 63, No. 4, 2021, https://journals.sagepub.com/doi/full/10.1177/00221856211035173.

3 Lyn Craig and Brendan Churchill, 'Working and caring at home: Gender differences in the effects of Covid-19 on paid and unpaid labor in Australia', *Feminist Economics*, Vol. 27, Nos. 1–2, 2021, https://www.tandfonline.com/doi/full/10.1080/13545701.2020.1831039.

4 Leonora Risse and Angela Jackson, 'A gender lens on the workforce impacts of the COVID-19 pandemic in Australia', *Australian Journal of Labour Economics*, Vol. 24, No. 2, 2021, https://research.curtin.edu.au/businesslaw/wp-content/uploads/sites/5/2021/10/AJLE242risse.pdf.

5 Kristine Ziwica, 'The data says it all: There's a significant "motherhood penalty" in Australia and it's getting worse', *Women's Agenda*, 4 April 2018, https://womensagenda.com.au/business/31938/.

6 Amy Remeikis, 'Morrison government failing women with lack of action on gender inequality in workforce, ACTU says', *The Guardian*, 20 September 2021, https://www.theguardian.com/australia-news/2021/sep/20/morrison-government-failing-women-with-lack-of-action-on-gender-inequality-in-workforce-actu-says.

7 Madeline Hislop, '"Very large fall" in female workforce participation rate in April, new figures show', *Women's Agenda*, 19 May 2021, https://womensagenda.com.au/latest/very-large-fall-in-female-workforce-participation-rate-in-april-new-figures-show/.
8 Kristine Ziwica, '"Joshonomics": How gullible does the Treasurer think women are?', *Women's Agenda*, 21 February 2022, https://womensagenda.com.au/latest/joshonomics-how-gullible-does-the-treasurer-think-women-are/.
9 Elizabeth Hill and Rae Cooper, 'Australia's working women are productivity gold. Here are five ways to help them thrive', *The Guardian*, 14 December 2021, https://www.theguardian.com/commentisfree/2021/dec/14/australias-working-women-are-productivity-gold-here-are-five-ways-to-help-them-thrive.
10 Deloitte Global, *Women @ Work: A Global Outlook: Australia Findings*, 2021, https://www2.deloitte.com/content/dam/Deloitte/au/Documents/about-deloitte/deloitte-au-about-women-work-global-outlook-210521.pdf.
11 Kristine Ziwica, '"It's a matter of holding ground": Where to for gender equality in 2020', *The Sydney Morning Herald*, 30 January 2020, https://www.smh.com.au/lifestyle/life-and-relationships/it-s-a-matter-of-holding-ground-where-to-for-gender-equality-in-2020-20200121-p53tgb.html.
12 World Economic Forum, *Global Gender Gap Report 2021*, 30 March 2021, https://www.weforum.org/reports/global-gender-gap-report-2021.
13 Joann Ellison Rodgers, 'Go forth in anger', *Psychology Today*, 11 March 2014, https://www.psychologytoday.com/au/articles/201403/go-forth-in-anger.
14 Susan Krauss Whitbourne, 'Why don't we trust angry women?', *Psychology Today*, 3 November 2015, https://www.psychologytoday.com/au/blog/fulfillment-any-age/201511/why-dont-we-trust-angry-women.
15 Rebecca Solnit, *Hope in the Dark: Untold Histories, Wild Possibilities*, New York: Nation Books, 2004.
16 Paul Karp, 'Australian Human Rights Commission to slash staff after budget cuts and surge in workload', *The Guardian*, 17 March 2022, https://www.theguardian.com/australia-news/2022/mar/17/australian-human-rights-commission-to-slash-staff-after-budget-cuts-and-surge-in-workload.

17 Paul Karp, 'Australian Human Rights Commission status at risk over Coalition's appointment process', *The Guardian*, 7 April 2022, https://www.theguardian.com/australia-news/2022/apr/07/australian-human-rights-commissions-status-at-risk-over-coalitions-appointment-process.

18 Kristine Ziwica, 'Scott Morrison and the women's movement', *The Saturday Paper*, 14 August 2021, https://www.thesaturdaypaper.com.au/news/politics/2021/08/14/scott-morrison-and-the-womens-movement/162886320012276.

19 Australian Human Rights Commission, *Supporting Working Parents: Pregnancy and Return to Work National Review – Report*, 25 July 2014, https://humanrights.gov.au/our-work/sex-discrimination/publications/supporting-working-parents-pregnancy-and-return-work?_ga=2.3481079.611517161.1651468387-174894530.1651468387.

20 Kristine Ziwica, 'Did Australian business leaders just pledge not to violate the most basic equal pay principle, and we're happy about it?', *Women's Agenda*, 28 August 2017, https://womensagenda.com.au/latest/soapbox/australian-business-leaders-just-pledge-not-violate-basic-equal-pay-principle-happy/.

21 Future Super, *Equality is Everyone's Business*, 2020, https://equalityiseveryonesbusiness.com.au/.

22 Constance Grady, 'The waves of feminism and why people keep fighting over them, explained', *Vox*, 20 July 2018, https://www.vox.com/2018/3/20/16955588/feminism-waves-explained-first-second-third-fourth.

23 Rebecca Walker, 'Becoming the Third Wave', *Ms.* magazine, Jan-Feb, 1992.

24 Sally Howard, *The Home Stretch: Why it's Time to Come Clean about Who Does the Dishes*, London: Atlantic Books, 2020.

25 Andi Zeisler, *We Were Feminists Once: From Riot Grrrl to Covergirl®, the Buying and Selling of a Political Movement*, New York: Public Affairs, 2016.

26 Lisa Belkin, 'The opt-out revolution', *The New York Times*, 26 October 2003, https://www.nytimes.com/2003/10/26/magazine/the-opt-out-revolution.html.

27 Judith Warner, "The opt-out generation wants back in", *The New York Times*, 7 August 2013, https://www.nytimes.com/2013/08/11/magazine/the-opt-out-generation-wants-back-in.html.

28 Linda R. Hirshman, *Get to Work … and Get a Life, Before it's Too Late*, New York: Viking Penguin, 2006.
29 Joan C. Williams, Jessica Manvell and Stephanie Bornstein, '"Opt out" or pushed out?: How the press covers work/family conflict', Center for WorkLife Law, 2006, https://www.psychologytoday.com/files/attachments/47131/optoutorpushedoutreportfinal.pdf.
30 Danielle Wood, Kate Griffiths and Tom Crowley, *Women's Work: The Impact of the COVID Crisis on Australian Women*, Grattan Institute, 2021, https://grattan.edu.au/report/womens-work/.
31 David Richardson and Richard Denniss, 'Gender experiences during the COVID-19 lockdown', Australia Institute, June 2020, https://australiainstitute.org.au/wp-content/uploads/2020/12/Gender-experience-during-the-COVID-19-lockdown.pdf.
32 Anne-Marie Slaughter, 'Rosie could be a riveter because of a care economy. Where is ours?', *The New York Times*, 16 April 2021, https://www.nytimes.com/2021/04/16/opinion/care-economy-infrastructure-rosie-the-riveter.html.
33 Sara Charlesworth and Linda Isherwood, 'Migrant aged-care workers in Australia: do they have poorer-quality jobs than their locally born counterparts?', *Ageing & Society*, Vol. 41, No. 3, 2020, https://doi.org/10.1017/S0144686X20000525
34 Silvia Federici, *Wages Against Housework*, London: Power of Women Collective, 1975.
35 Anne Manne, 'Making women's unpaid work count', *The Monthly*, May 2018, https://www.themonthly.com.au/issue/2018/may/1525096800/anne-manne/making-women-s-unpaid-work-count.
36 Workplace Gender Equality Agency, *Unpaid Care Work and the Labour Market*, 9 November 2016, https://www.wgea.gov.au/sites/default/files/documents/australian-unpaid-care-work-and-the-labour-market.pdf.
37 PwC, *Understanding the Unpaid Economy*, March 2017, https://www.pwc.com.au/australia-in-transition/publications/understanding-the-unpaid-economy-mar17.pdf.
38 Emily Peck, 'Policymakers used to ignore child care. Then came the pandemic', *The New York Times*, 6 October 2021, https://www.nytimes.com/2021/05/09/business/child-care-infrastructure-biden.html.

39 Ai-jen Poo, *The Age of Dignity: Preparing for the Elder Boom in a Changing America*, New York: The New Press, 2015.

40 CompliSpace Aged Care, *A Perfect Storm: What's Driving Australia's Aged Care Crisis*, 2021, https://www.complispace.com.au/workforce-report-2021.

41 Deloitte Australia, 'Pandemic postscript: Working women face alarmingly high levels of burnout despite shifting work arrangements' (media release), 9 May 2022, https://www2.deloitte.com/au/en/pages/media-releases/articles/women-at-work-outlook-060522.html; Deloitte Australia, *2022 Women @ Work Report*, 9 May 2022, https://www2.deloitte.com/au/en/pages/media-releases/articles/women-at-work-outlook-060522.html.

42 Multicultural Centre for Women's Health and Gender Equity Victoria, *Left Behind: Migrant and Refugee Women's Experiences of COVID-19*, 6 October 2021, https://www.genvic.org.au/focus-areas/genderequalhealth/left-behind-migrant-and-refugee-womens-experiences-of-covid-19/.

43 Lydia Saad, Sangeeta Agrawal and Ben Wigert, *Gender Gap in Worker Burnout Widened Amid the Pandemic*, Gallup, 27 December 2021, https://www.gallup.com/workplace/358349/gender-gap-worker-burnout-widened-amid-pandemic.aspx.

44 Colleen Ammerman and Boris Groysber, 'Women can't go back to the pre-pandemic status quo', *Harvard Business Review*, 8 March 2022, https://hbr.org/2022/03/women-cant-go-back-to-the-pre-pandemic-status-quo.

45 Olivia Evans, *Gari Yala (Speak the Truth): Gendered Insights*, Workplace Gender Equality Agency, Jumbunna Institute for Indigenous Education and Research, and Diversity Council Australia, 2021, https://www.wgea.gov.au/sites/default/files/documents/Gari_Yala_genderedinsights2021.pdf.

46 Catherine Archer and Women of Colour Australia (WoCA), *Women of Colour Australia: Workplace Survey 2021*, WoCA, 2021, https://womenofcolour.org.au/workplace-survey-report-2021/#.

47 Jane O'Leary, Dimitria Groutsis and Rose D'Almada-Remedios, *Cracking the Glass-Cultural Ceiling*, Diversity Council Australia, September 2017, https://www.dca.org.au/sites/default/files/synopsis_-_cracking_the_glass-cultural_ceiling.pdf.

48 Women with Disabilities Australia, *National Disability Employment Strategy Consultation Paper: Women With Disabilities Australia Submission*, May 2021, https://engage.dss.gov.au/wp-content/uploads/2021/06/WWDA_NDES_May2021_FINAL.pdf.

49 Pooja Lakshmin, 'How society has turned its back on mothers', *The New York Times*, 4 February 2021, https://www.nytimes.com/2021/02/04/parenting/working-mom-burnout-coronavirus.html.

50 Women's Agenda, 'Are we seeing the Great Resignation or the Great Exhaustion?', *Women's Agenda*, 10 March 2022, https://womensagenda.com.au/latest/are-we-seeing-the-great-resignation-or-the-great-exhaustion/.

51 Jennifer Moss, 'Burnout is about your workplace, not your people', *Harvard Business Review*, 11 December 2019, https://hbr.org/2019/12/burnout-is-about-your-workplace-not-your-people.

52 Lean In, *Women in the Workplace 2021*, https://leanin.org/women-in-the-workplace-report-2021/introduction, 2021; NPR, 'The Great Resignation' (transcript), 22 October 2021, https://www.npr.org/transcripts/1048332481; FRED Economic Data, 'Labor force participation rate – Women', 6 May 2022, https://fred.stlouisfed.org/series/LNS11300002; Don Lee, 'Women put careers on hold during COVID to care for kids. They may never recover', *Los Angeles Times*, 18 August 2021, https://www.latimes.com/politics/story/2021-08-18/pandemic-pushes-moms-to-scale-back-or-quit-their-careers.

53 Women's Agenda, *Women's Agenda Ambition Report*, 2021, https://womensagenda.com.au/wp-content/uploads/2021/10/Womens_Ambition-Report_by_Womens_Agenda.pdf.

54 Deloitte, *Women @ Work: A Global Outlook: Australia Findings*.

55 Lisa Annese, 'Inclusion at work – an antidote to the great resignation', Diversity Council Australia, 9 December 2021, https://www.dca.org.au/media-releases/inclusion-work-antidote-great-resignation.

56 Dan Nahum, *Working from Home, or Living at Work?*, Centre for Future Work, November 2021, https://d3n8a8pro7vhmx.cloudfront.net/theausinstitute/pages/3901/attachments/original/1637029639/Go_Home_On_Time_Day_2021_FINAL.pdf?1637029639.

57 National Museum of Australia, 'Equal pay for women', https://www.nma.gov.au/defining-moments/resources/equal-pay-for-women.

58 Miriam Glennie, Anna von Reibnitz, Jananie William, Sally Curtis and Sarbari Bordia, *Gender Pay Gap Reporting in Australia: Time for an Upgrade*, Australian National University, October 2021, https://giwl.anu.edu.au/research/publications/gender-pay-gap-reporting-australia-time-upgrade.

59 Jennifer Duke, 'Gender pay gap to remain for decades without fast improvement, data shows', *The Age*, 26 November 2020, https://www.theage.com.au/politics/federal/gender-pay-gap-to-remain-for-decades-without-fast-improvement-wgea-20201125-p56hpu.html.

60 Wendy Tuohy, '"This is laying the groundwork for some pretty serious poverty for women"', *The Age*, 24 May 2020, https://www.theage.com.au/lifestyle/gender/this-is-laying-the-groundwork-for-some-pretty-serious-poverty-for-women-20200522-p54vp0.html.

61 Bankwest Curtin Economics Centre, 'Over a quarter of a century until the gender pay gap likely to close', 25 March 2021, https://bcec.edu.au/media/over-a-quarter-of-a-century-until-gender-pay-gap-likely-to-close/.

62 KPMG, Diversity Council Australia, and Workplace Gender Equality Agency, *She's Price(d)less: The Economics of the Gender Pay Gap*, 22 August 2019, https://www.wgea.gov.au/sites/default/files/documents/She%27s-Price%28d%29less-2019-Detailed-report_0.pdf.

63 Benjamin Artz, Amanda H. Goodall and Andrew J. Oswald, 'Do women ask?', *Industrial Relations*, 9 May 2018, https://onlinelibrary.wiley.com/doi/abs/10.1111/irel.12214.

64 Emily T. Amanatullah and Catherine H. Tinsley, 'Punishing female negotiators for asserting too much … or not enough: Exploring why advocacy moderates backlash against assertive female negotiators', *Organizational Behavior and Human Decision Process*, Vol. 120, No. 1, 2013, https://www.sciencedirect.com/science/article/abs/pii/S0749597812000416.

65 Victoria L. Brescoll and Eric Luis Uhlmann, 'Can an angry woman get ahead? Status conferral, gender, and expression of emotion in the workplace', *Psychological Science*, Vol. 19, No. 3, 2008, https://journals.sagepub.com/doi/full/10.1111/j.1467-9280.2008.02079.x.

66 VitalSmarts, 'Women judged more harshly than men when speaking up assertively', 2015, http://www.norskstyrebase.no/uploads/9/4/6/7/9467257/014_gender-inequality.pdf.
67 Joan C. Williams, 'Women, work and the art of gender judo', *The Washington Post*, 24 January 2014, https://www.washingtonpost.com/opinions/women-work-and-the-art-of-gender-judo/2014/01/24/29e209b2-82b2-11e3-8099-9181471f7aaf_story.html.
68 Glennie et al., *Gender Pay Gap Reporting in Australia*.
69 Department of the Prime Minister and Cabinet, *WGEA Review Report: Review of the Workplace Gender Equality Act 2012*, December 2021, https://www.pmc.gov.au/resource-centre/office-women/wgea-review-report.
70 Owain Emslie, Danielle Wood and Kate Griffiths, 'Reform "daddy leave" to narrow the gender gap in paid and unpaid work', Grattan Institute, 10 August 2020, https://grattan.edu.au/news/reform-daddy-leave-to-narrow-the-gender-gap-in-paid-and-unpaid-work/.
71 Oxfam, 'Why the majority of the world's poor are women', 8 March 2017, https://www.oxfam.org.au/2017/03/why-the-majority-of-the-worlds-poor-are-women/.
72 Gemma Hartley, 'Women aren't nags – we're just fed up', *Harpers Bazaar*, 27 September 2017, https://www.harpersbazaar.com/culture/features/a12063822/emotional-labor-gender-equality/.
73 Zoe Daniel, 'How coronavirus has changed the roles in the family home', ABC News, 13 May 2020, https://www.abc.net.au/news/2020–05–13/coronavirus-has-changed-roles-in-family-home/12239542.
74 Titan Alon, Matthias Doepke, Jane Olmstead-Rumsey and Michèle Tertilt, *The Impact of COVID-19 on Gender Equality*, National Bureau of Economic Research, 2020, https://www.nber.org/papers/w26947.
75 Craig and Churchill, 'Working and caring at home'.
76 Craig and Churchill, 'Working and caring at home'.
77 Craig and Churchill, 'Working and caring at home'.
78 Australian Bureau of Statistics, 'Household impacts of COVID-19 survey', December 2020, https://www.abs.gov.au/statistics/people/people-and-communities/household-impacts-covid-19-survey/dec-2020#unpaid-work.

79 Deloitte Global, *Women @ Work: A Global Outlook: Australia Findings.*
80 OECD, *The Pursuit of Gender Equality: An Uphill Battle*, 4 October 2017, https://www.oecd.org/gender/the-pursuit-of-gender-equality-9789264281318-en.htm.
81 Women Deliver, *Citizens Call for a Gender-Equal World: A Roadmap for Action*, January 2021, https://womendeliver.org/wp-content/uploads/2021/02/Global_Report_English.pdf.
82 Annabel Crabb, *The Wife Drought: Why Women Need Wives and Men Need Lives*, Sydney: Random House, 2014.
83 Nikki van der Gaag, Brian Heilman, Taveeshi Gupta, Ché Nembhard and Gary Barker, *State of the World's Fathers*, MenCare, 8 February 2019, https://men-care.org/2019/02/08/state-of-the-worlds-fathers-report-to-launch-june-2019-in-advance-of-fathers-day/.
84 Evrim Altintas and Oriel Sullivan, 'Fifty years of change updated: Cross-national gender convergence in housework', *Demographic Research*, Vol. 35, Art. 16, 2016, https://www.demographic-research.org/volumes/vol35/16/35-16.pdf.
85 Amanda Barroso and Juliana Menasce Horowitz, 'The pandemic has highlighted many challenges for mothers, but they aren't necessarily new', Pew Research Center, 17 March 2021, https://www.pewresearch.org/fact-tank/2021/03/17/the-pandemic-has-highlighted-many-challenges-for-mothers-but-they-arent-necessarily-new/.
86 van der Gaag et al., *State of the World's Fathers.*
87 Judy Syfers Brady, '"I want a wife": The timeless feminist manifesto', *The Cut*, 22 November 2017, https://www.thecut.com/2017/11/i-want-a-wife-by-judy-brady-syfers-new-york-mag-1971.html.
88 Crabb, *The Wife Drought.*
89 Sally Howard, *The Home Stretch: Why it's Time to Come Clean about Who Does the Dishes,* London: Atlantic Books, 2021.
90 Barbara Ehrenreich, *Nickel and Dimed: On (Not) Getting By in America,* New York: Metropolitan Books, 2001.
91 Arlie Hochschild, *The Second Shift: Working Families and the Revolution at Home,* New York: Viking Penguin, 1989.
92 Claire Cain Miller, 'Millennial men aren't the dads they thought they'd be', *The New York Times*, 30 July 2015, https://www.nytimes.com/2015/07/31/upshot/millennial-men-find-work-and-family-hard-to-balance.html.

93 David S. Pedulla and Sarah Thébaud, 'Can we finish the revolution?: Gender, work-family ideals and institutional constraint', *American Sociological Review*, Vol. 8, No. 1, 2015, https://journals.sagepub.com/doi/abs/10.1177/0003122414564008.

94 Workplace Gender Equality Agency, 'Employers need to care more about carers', 22 November 2018, https://www.wgea.gov.au/newsroom/employers-need-to-care-more-about-carers.

95 Kate Higgins, 'Men twice as likely to have flexible work requests knocked back: study', ABC News, 3 February 2016, https://www.abc.net.au/news/2016-02-03/men-more-likely-to-have-flexible-work-requests-knocked-back/7137208.

96 Higgins, 'Men twice as likely to have flexible work requests knocked back'.

97 Marian Baird, Myra Hamilton and Andreea Constantin, 'Gender equality and paid parental leave in Australia: A decade of giant leaps or baby steps?', *Journal of Industrial Relations*, Vol. 63, No. 4, 2021, https://journals.sagepub.com/doi/abs/10.1177/00221856211008219.

98 Annabel Crabb, 'Men at work: Australia's parenthood trap', *Quarterly Essay*, No. 75, September 2019, https://www.quarterlyessay.com.au/essay/2019/09/men-at-work.

99 OECD Family Database, 'Family database: Indicator PF 3.4', May 2022, https://www.oecd.org/els/family/database.htm.

100 Miranda Stewart, Angela Jackson and Leonora Risse, 'If governments were really concerned about tax and the cost of living they would cut the cost of childcare', *The Conversation*, 13 May 2022, https://theconversation.com/if-governments-were-really-concerned-about-tax-and-the-cost-of-living-they-would-cut-the-cost-of-childcare-182669.

101 Australian Bureau of Statistics, 'Barriers and incentives to labour force participation, Australia: Factors that influence how people participate in the labour market and the hours they work', 28 August 2020, https://www.abs.gov.au/statistics/labour/employment-and-unemployment/barriers-and-incentives-labour-force-participation-australia/latest-release.

102 Lisa Bryant, 'We must stop growth of corporate childcare that puts profits above children', *The Age*, 6 October 2021, https://www.theage.com.au/national/nsw/we-must-stop-growth-of-corporate-childcare-that-puts-profits-above-children-20211006-p58xqk.html.

103 Lisa Bryant, 'Childcare is on the ropes – and nurses and doctors can't work without it', *The Sydney Morning Herald*, 2 April 2020, https://www.theage.com.au/national/childcare-is-on-the-ropes-and-nurses-and-doctors-can-t-work-without-it-20200401-p54fzy.html.

104 Department of Education, Skills and Employment, *Early Childhood Education and Care Relief Package Four Week Review*, 18 May 2020, https://www.dese.gov.au/early-childhood/resources/early-childhood-education-and-care-relief-package-four-week-review.

105 Dan Tehan, 'ABC Afternoon Briefing with Patricia Karvelas' (transcript), 2 April 2020, https://ministers.dese.gov.au/tehan/abc-afternoon-briefing-patricia-karvelas.

106 Kristine Ziwica, 'We can learn a thing or two from the communists about childcare', *The Sydney Morning Herald*, 2 May 2019, https://www.smh.com.au/national/we-can-learn-a-thing-or-two-from-the-communists-about-childcare-20190501-p51iwt.html.

107 Rhaina Cohen, 'Who took care of Rosie the Riveter's kids?', *The Atlantic*, November 2015, https://www.theatlantic.com/business/archive/2015/11/daycare-world-war-rosie-riveter/415650/.

108 Quentin Brummet et al., 'Rosie's kids: Pre-school exposure during WWII and later-life outcomes', United States Census Bureau, 28 July 2017, http://conference.nber.org/confer/2017/SI2017/CH/Ferrie_Brummet_Goldin_Olivetti_Horner_Rolf.pdf.

109 Chris M. Herbst, 'Universal child care, maternal employment, and children's long-run outcomes: Evidence from the U.S. Lanham Act of 1940', IZA Discussion Paper Series, December 2013, https://ftp.iza.org/dp7846.pdf.

110 Bryce Covert, 'America's child care crisis is an economic crisis', *The New York Times*, 26 June 2019, https://www.nytimes.com/2019/06/26/opinion/democratic-debate-child-care.html.

111 Kate Noble and Peter Hurley, *Counting the Cost to Families: Assessing Childcare Affordability in Australia*, Mitchell Institute, Victoria University, 2021, https://www.vu.edu.au/sites/default/files/mitchell-institute-assessing-childcare-affordability-in-Australia.pdf.

112 Peter Hurley, Hannah Matthews and Sue Pennicuik, *Deserts and Oases: How Accessible Is Childcare in Australia?*, Mitchell Institute, Victoria University, 2022, https://www.vu.edu.au/sites/default/files/how-accessible-is-childcare-report.pdf.

113 Rob Bray, Ben Phillips, Ilan Katz and Matthew Gray, 'The 2018 childcare package was partly designed to help families work more, but the benefits were too modest to matter', *The Conversation*, 29 March 2022, https://theconversation.com/the-2018-childcare-package-was-partly-designed-to-help-families-work-more-but-the-benefits-were-too-modest-to-matter-179934.

114 Josh Butler, '$15-a-day childcare, changes to paid parental leave under new government plan', *HuffPost*, 7 February 2017, https://www.huffpost.com/archive/au/entry/15-a-day-childcare-changes-to-paid-parental-leave-under-new-go_a_21709175.

115 Wendy Tuohy, 'Philanthropist leads call to lift women's lagging economic security', *The Sydney Morning Herald*, 24 November 2021, https://www.smh.com.au/national/philanthropist-leads-call-to-lift-women-s-lagging-economic-security-20211124-p59bsm.html.

116 Women with Disabilities Australia, *National Disability Employment Strategy Consultation Paper: Women With Disabilities Australia Submission.*

117 Australian Human Rights Commission, *Everyone's Business: Fourth National Survey on Sexual Harassment in Australian Workplaces*, September 2018, https://humanrights.gov.au/our-work/sex-discrimination/publications/everyones-business-fourth-national-survey-sexual.

118 Australian Human Rights Commission, *Everyone's Business.*

119 Marian Baird, Rae Cooper, Elizabeth Hill, Elspeth Probyn and Ariadne Vromen, 2018, *Women and the Future of Work*, University of Sydney, https://ses.library.usyd.edu.au/bitstream/handle/2123/21254/women-and-the-future-of-work.pdf.

120 Australian Human Rights Commission, *Respect@Work: Sexual Harassment National Inquiry Report*, 2020, https://humanrights.gov.au/our-work/sex-discrimination/publications/respectwork-sexual-harassment-national-inquiry-report-2020.

121 Ariane Hegewisch, Jessica Forden and Eve Mefferd, *Paying Today and Tomorrow: Charting the Financial Costs of Sexual Harassment*, Institute for Women's Policy Research and Time's Up Foundation, 2021, https://iwpr.org/wp-content/uploads/2021/07/Paying-Today-and-Tomorrow_Charting-the-Financial-Costs-of-Workplace-Sexual-Harassment_FINAL.pdf.

122 Catherine Marriott [@roseycatherine], 'I have no words for how frustrated, hopeless, sad.... words escape me... I am at this! ...' [tweet], Twitter, 2 September 2021, https://twitter.com/roseycatherine/status/1433383322403495939.

123 Australian Human Rights Commission, *Set the Standard: Report on the Independent Review into Commonwealth Parliamentary Workplaces*, 2021, https://humanrights.gov.au/set-standard-2021.

124 Minnesota Public Radio, 'Poll: Nearly half of the women who experienced sexual harassment leave their jobs or switch careers', Marketplace, 2018, https://www.marketplace.org/2018/03/09/new-numbers-reflect-lasting-effects-workplace-harassment-women/.

125 Australian Government, *Women's Budget Statement 2022–23*, 29 March 2022, https://budget.gov.au/2022-23/content/womens-statement/download/womens_budget_statement_2022-23.pdf.

126 Nick Cater and Nicolle Flint, *Gender and Politics: A Menzies Research Centre Discussion Paper*, Menzies Research Centre, 2015.

127 Matthew Doran, 'Tony Abbott supports targets for female representation in Liberal Party as report highlights lack of women', ABC News, 15 August 2015, https://www.abc.net.au/news/2015-08-15/liberals-urged-to-attract-women-into-parliament/6699818.

128 Kristine Ziwica, 'We're getting a "bloke-covery" response to a "she-cession": How will women respond at the ballot box?', *Women's Agenda*, 9 July 2020, https://womensagenda.com.au/latest/were-getting-a-bloke-covery-response-to-a-she-cession-how-will-women-respond-at-the-ballot-box/.

129 Jenna Price, 'Shifting preferences: Why women voters may swing the election', *The Sydney Morning Herald*, 23 February 2022, https://www.smh.com.au/politics/federal/shifting-preferences-why-women-voters-may-swing-the-election-20220222-p59yhk.html.